The God of Evil

Other books by Frederick Sontag

The God of Evil:

An Argument from the Existence of the Devil

FREDERICK SONTAG

at least, a fresh approach to the subject of theology —

First, he shows the inadequacy of atheism, existentialism, scientism, "God is dead" etc, then he begins a reconstruction

A Gospel Tract for the atheist

The author takes to scientific, empirical, experiential approach to G-d here — the undeniable facts of life are his starting point

HARPER & ROW, PUBLISHERS

NEW YORK, EVANSTON, AND LONDON

1817

FIRST EDITION

LIBRARY OF CONGRESS CATALOG CARD NUMBER: 70-109887

For

A.B.S.D.

"This is to be called woman,
for this was taken from man."
—Genesis 2:23

We assiduously avoid investigating whether in the very power of <u>evil</u> God might not have placed some special purpose which it is most important for us to kn<u>o</u>w.

Know evil well to know God

C. G. Jung in PSYCHOLOGY AND ALCHEMY

Preface

If anything is clear in theology today, it is that we need to uncover a new basis for our thinking about God, and that this should be one which is both novel but still not inconsistent with our traditional notions of God. The suggestion of this book is that atheism may provide the needed ground for this construction. In starting to write about atheism, it was not my original intention to uncover a new view of God. It is just that, as I thought more and more about the contemporary sources of atheism, I discovered why some concepts of God cannot stand up against these forces, but I also decided that a God might be found who could. If the force of evil is the main source of atheism, the God which atheism can lead us to will have to be a "God of Evil."

Any value which the reader may find in this new basis for thinking about God owes much to the patience of the class who first read and commented on my original lectures. During 1966–67 I was invited to be the first non-Catholic to lecture regularly in a Roman seminary, and, in line with these revolutionary times, the title suggested to me for the series of lectures was "The Problem of Atheism." As these lectures progressed, while I was in residence at the Benedectine house in Rome—the Collegio di Sant' Anselmo—a new theme of "the God of atheism" began to emerge. Thus, I owe an apology as well as a debt of gratitude to the Roman seminarians who came to listen and then stayed to comment on those lectures. These students helped their teacher during a confusing time of transition, that is, while a God began to emerge from the problem of atheism and its source in the constantly disturbing fact of the power of evil.

Mrs. Gloria DeLia typed all the draft of the lectures for mimeographed distribution to the seminarians in Rome. However, a comparison of those lectures, which lie bound in the Waldensian Seminary Library in Rome, with this present book would indicate how many evolutions the original topic has gone through in order to reach its present form. Mrs. Barbara Benton of Claremont typed two successive versions, each of which differed greatly from its predecessor. It is not easy to find a God in atheism and evil. As the new thesis gradually emerged from the original problem, the author finally had to cut it loose from the series of lectures in order to set a new God free.

Since this is only one of four series of lectures delivered in Rome that year, all those who made possible such an unusual invitation and who contributed to its success have been acknowledged in print before. Thanking them all once again is only right, although it still will not repay the debt. If some new insight into God was gained in a monastery setting, that in itself is the best possible repayment. Since monks devote themselves to "seeking God in community," this would also be a very fitting consequence for monastic life in a time of atheism when evil seems more real than God.

FREDERICK SONTAG

Claremont, California
December 25, 1969

Contents

Contents

The God of Evil

CHAPTER I

The Argument Away from the Existence of God

The death of God has been announced in every era and not just in our own. Why is this message repeated so continually? You would think that man, who has achieved so much in science and technology, would have taken a definite stand on this issue long ago. Various arguments for the existence of God, as well as the missionary effort of the churches, have been at work for centuries. Many philosophers have attempted to decide this question once and for all, but none has achieved universal acceptance. It is not because God has lacked either advocates or detractors that the case for his existence has not long ago been decided conclusively. There must, then, be powerful and persistent arguments for atheism which never disappear. Are there factors, not insubstantial, which work against affirming the existence of any God, even if these forces are not quite strong enough to settle the matter once and for all?

Sometimes we learn a great deal by letting our minds follow one of the proofs for God's existence. Yet it might be even more instructive to consider in detail the problem of atheism and to ask: What are those built-in factors which seem so continually and so successfully to work against a belief in God? The resulting answer will not be an examination of some particular form of atheism but instead a more radical investigation: The attempt to determine what permanent and forceful features of our world

$= \chi$

1

and existence (e.g., evil) are at the root of the constant tendency which moves so many men away from God and toward atheism.

This present examination of the sources of atheism is admittedly different from most. Atheistic arguments are usually negative and destructive, perhaps with justification as we shall see. Driven by some compelling experience, most assertions of atheism aim to deny forcefully the existence of God. Our intent is not to consider one particular argument from among the many negative ones, but rather to conduct an examination of the sources that continually give rise to them. The aim is not to conclude the debate, either temporarily or permanently, but to see if we can form a possible concept of God from the very sources of the arguments against him, and from the fact that they do actually have such a firm and constant ground for assertion. Can we learn anything new about God by examining the origins of the denial of his existence? This is an attempt at a new *via negativa*.

We could easily have been placed in a world which had no factors that support atheism, and then determining God's existence would be a simple matter. Any God who does exist, then, must be such as to account for the existence of the arguments against him, since he placed them in the world in deciding to create it as he did. Thus, if any concept of God is incapable of accounting for the existence of the factors that argue against him, it cannot really describe God, since the forces leading toward atheism are very real and would have to have been created willingly and knowingly by any God worthy of his name. God must have designed intentionally both atheism and the grounds for it. To ask what kind of God would do this and why—this is surely to learn something important about God.

Recent metaphysics has taken an interesting approach to the positive via the negative in seeking to reveal the structure of Being through an examination of Nonbeing.* This same indirect route may be possible where God is concerned. He cannot be seen, but the elements that argue against God certainly are felt with immediate force, and they may actually form a more con-

*See my *The Existentialist Prolegomena: To a Future Metaphysics* (Chicago: University of Chicago Press, 1969).

2

Nonbeing certainly cannot acct for being —

So God — is basis to evil

14

True

crete source of information for us. As Plato pointed out in the *Sophist*, Being must account for the existence of Nonbeing, so that any valid concept of God ought to include an account of the arguments against his existence. Why not, then, begin to build a concept of God precisely at that point?

We do not, of course, begin *de novo* here. In our philosophical and theological literature there exists a continual stream of arguments for God's existence, plus a variety of concepts of God's nature. Although a majority of classical philosophers offer arguments for God's existence, there are many persuasive arguments for naturalism too. It may be that negative arguments seem stronger at the time but do not last, while positive construction tends to establish itself in the inherited literature. In any case, negative arguments appear to be stronger today, and they create a pressing problem even within religious circles. Thus, both positive and negative approaches to God give us a context for our consideration much more substantial than random or individual impressions.

Interesting

This is the function of philosophy, i.e., to take a current problem such as atheism and set it in an accumulated tradition for consideration. Where atheism is concerned, our approach today may well involve certain important novelties, but we must make these clear and elaborate them into a fixed form. We can do this by adding the insights of our day and its strongest impressions to the inherited philosophical tradition. Where God is concerned, what we need is to find such a structured context, since our own immediate impressions are insufficient. The context of the inherited classical arguments does give order to our considerations, although our major task is to reshape the tradition in order to accommodate the impressions of a new day. In our case, this seems to mean beginning with evil and atheism and their origins and asking what the negative can tell us about the positive, since these are the strongest features of our time.

It may be that you cannot have a God without having a Devil, i.e., a symbol for the negative and destructive forces which are loose in the world. In this case, two alternatives are always open to us where God is concerned. We may form a positive concept of God from his acknowledged perfections (e.g., goodness) as

3

these are present in the world, and then work hard to give the Devil the reality due to him; or, on the other hand, we may simply start with the Devil. If we concentrate upon the negative forces active in the world, we may easily combine them into one "center for destruction" and let the Devil obscure God. Yet, since life is not all violence, we can also start from the accumulated negative elements and build from them an account of a God who can exist in spite of such destructive forces—one whose existence is commensurate with the presence of strong negativity.

This is the argument from the existence of the Devil, but whether it will yield two Gods or only one it is impossible to know in advance. However, the virtue of beginning with the Devil is that he often is much more real to most men, and you are not burdened at the beginning of the argument with a fixed concept of God which may only have to be changed in the light of actual experience. Just as the crazy man may teach us much about sanity, so beginning with the Devil may be a better guide to God today than any positive idea of God could be.

Although men still continue to examine the various arguments for the existence of God, in recent times the movement of thought has been primarily "away from God." This is true not so much in the sense of religious atheism (i.e., those who reject religion) as it is in the more interesting fact that, where philosophical thought is concerned, men have shied from a direct approach to God intellectually. What is fascinating here is that this has been true even of the theologians.

The contrast is striking. Once theologians apparently moved easily and without misgiving to construct theories of the divine nature and then to discuss the fascinating problems that develop in this process, due to the transcendence of ordinary categories. God is still considered by theologians today, but the approach is hesitant, tentative, and seldom very detailed. God often enters theology only by having his name mentioned, or by a reference at the end. At best he is an inference from human anthropology.

If this tendency is to be reversed—if some men find the existence of evil a reason for denying God's existence—then our concept of God must be altered to render a more adequate account of evil. If in looking at life some men see no evidence for God, we must begin by examining what "evidence" means in this instance and decide according to what standards of evidence God may be said to exist. If others find no need to postulate a God in order to explain the natural world, we need to examine the meanings of *to explain*. Most important, we must learn what concept of God, if introduced, might have more explanatory power—e.g., why so much suffering in the world?

If some find the abuses of religion a reason for denying God, we must be sure that we construct a concept which detaches God sufficiently from human error. We must neither identify him with religious excess nor remove him from religious practice altogether. As should be evident, there is no necessity to yield to every negative argument and simply accept its assumptions; but it may be extremely instructive to examine the premises upon which any line of reasoning rejects God. Since we have some flexibility in working out a definition of God, these negative arguments are helpful in deciding which attributes are important for a new concept of God. For instance, we must include positive attributes which do not exclude the negative factors present in our experience of men and the world.

In giving arguments for God's existence, positive evidence seeks to produce a certain reasoning which guides the mind to affirm this. In our case, negative reasoning now becomes a ground upon which positive qualities may be developed by way of contrast. The reasons why a man does not do something may be as instructive as the reasons for which he takes a positive action. In a sense we learn more about a man when we discover why he does not act than we learn from what he does in fact do. Hamlet's failure to act is more revealing—and more crucial—than anything he does. God has done certain things (if he exists), but recently we have learned that there are a great number of things which he has not done, and such nonelections are perhaps more revealing of the divine intent. The arguments against God's existence may highlight what he has not done (e.g., to create better worlds), and why, and thus illuminate his nature more than reasoning based upon the world he did create.

It is significant that God's nonexistence is seldom taken either

5

casually or lightly. Some men rejoice over his "death," as Nietzsche does, since his absence from the scene implies greater power for man. Others may regret it, as Sartre does, because it removes the ethical source of judgment, guidance, and forgiveness. A few do pass over God lightly, but most who bother to deny his existence do so explicitly. The issue is a momentous one, and it is often surrounded by considerable feeling. Let us not ignore strong feeling; it may be our best guide to God.

Useful as God would be ethically, Sartre rejects him in the interest of freedom. What does this tell us about what God could and should not be like? The issue here is: Can a concept of God be devised which does not compromise human freedom? Nietzsche admires God's power and will but thinks that his existence would restrict man's creative power too much. The lesson to be learned here is: Can a human creativity be defined which is enhanced by a concept of God rather than curtailed by it?

Another interesting reversal would be to ask what would happen to a philosophical theory that led to a denial of God's existence if in fact God did exist? Few would contend that God is caused to exist or forced out of existence simply by an argument; his existence is independent of any such consideration. Thus, one possibility is that God does in fact exist in spite of Nietzsche's objections, Sartre's denial, and Hume's skepticism. If this were so, what would happen to their theories? In other words, is the theory so constructed that, if God did exist, his existence would force the author materially to alter the theory? If so, we may learn something interesting about both God and that theory.

Of course, if God exists but remains unknown, this may not change much. That, too, would be interesting to consider in any theory about God. If God's existence in one form would change Sartre's assertions (e.g., about ethical responsibility) while his existence in another way would not, we have learned something about the possibilities to be considered in any attempt to describe the divine nature. Certain factors may lead to a rejection of one concept of God, but these same negative factors can then be used to mold a concept of God which is not incompatible with other parts of that theory, e.g., with human freedom as Sartre defines it.

At this point some account must be given of the technical objections which can be raised against any description of God at all. Although they are actually less interesting and helpful than positive denials, still these prohibitions have been effective, and they may also be instructive for our attempt at negative construction. Kant is the name one usually thinks of first, and it is probably true that the Kantian theory of knowledge has placed more restrictions on new theological construction than any other. The first issue this raises is the question of the priority of epistemology itself. If an account of the knowing process must first be given, and if this is done through an analysis of the knower himself, the human subject automatically becomes the criterion for what can and cannot be done. Epistemology is 'first philosophy.' "Why shouldn't epistemology be our first consideration?" you may ask, but the fact is that both determining this priority and finding a beginning place for philosophy are crucial to the outcome of theology.

God has always been said to possess knowledge in a manner different from men and to be of such a nature that he does not appear within the process of knowing—at least in ordinary knowledge. Thus, when the Kantian starting point is accepted, knowledge of God is made difficult if not impossible. In setting the limits of knowledge by a study of man, God is immediately excluded, particularly in a day when men are by nature more atheistic than religious. Upon what basis can we assert that the knowing process of man does not provide us with the starting point for all philosophy? This question will not be treated directly here, except that the concept of God formed may yield the basis for an answer to it.

What we learn from these restrictions on talk about God, then, is that if you want to argue to God, it may require a different starting point. Is this possible, and why didn't Kant start there, since he admitted his desire to reach a knowledge of God? By way of an answer, consider this: At least one other potential starting point is to agree that knowledge is shaped, not by its own process, but by the mode of existence of its object. This classical

7

approach again makes metaphysics "first philosophy," since in order to understand modes of knowledge we must first come to a decision regarding possible modes of Being; Being defines the modes of knowledge of it. God is certainly one possible mode of Being; if you begin in this way, knowledge of God at least remains possible. If his mode of Being can be outlined satisfactorily, that will define the mode of knowledge applicable to him, even if the possible concepts of God remain plural because his Being can be described in more ways than one.

Kant, of course, was not ignorant of this procedure. In fact, he knew it all too well, and it was his specific intention to object to it and replace it with the priority of an epistemology of the knowing self. Upon what did his objections to this classical view of the priority of metaphysics rest, and what can we learn by studying his argument away from God?

Kant, like all moderns, wanted necessity and certainty in his theories, for he saw this, or thought he saw it, as an assumption of modern science. He accepted a concept of the development of theory such that modern theories invalidate previous procedures. He wanted philosophy to parallel science, and he felt that philosophy, too, must seek certainty, necessity,* and finality in its theory. On the other hand, if epistemology is a dependent enterprise—i.e., if it is deduced from the modes of Being discovered in your metaphysics—then philosophy is excluded from ever achieving a fully necessary theory.

If we return to a classical view of the priority of Being over knowledge, philosophy becomes a different kind of enterprise; now it will have to be plural in theory and always unfinished. Why should this be, and is this a situation we must accept or one against which we too should object? Kant, of course, did not think we should accept this consequence without a struggle. He correctly saw that the derivation of modes of knowledge from modes of Being always leaves us with the possibility that there are modes other than those we have uncovered. Or—almost

---

*'Necessity' means that the thing in question could not be other than it is, and 'certainty' results because the mind understands this ontological situation to be without alternative. 'Finality' is, thus, possible in theory if the structure of things can be characterized in this way.

worse—there may be some modes (e.g., God's) of such a nature that they exceed our complete grasp in any form of knowing. Finality, if it is to be achieved, must come by means of a restrictive theory of knowledge, i.e., one that sets limits on its goals and is so constructed that it is self-contained and achievable. Our first question is: Must philosophy begin by restricting its scope?

If we can surrender certainty and necessity, as Kant thought we could not, we are free to return to a metaphysics that allows us to approach God, even if it cannot guarantee this result. At least this possibility is now open to us, whereas with Kant it was not. Kant thought we must seek necessity and certainty; but can these be dispensed with? The first thing to point out is that even the restrictions imposed by Kant—or any later philosopher— seem to have failed to achieve that goal. Why? There are at least two answers, one external and one internal. Internally, our age has made the fascinating discovery that complete consistency without internal contradiction either cannot easily be achieved or at least cannot be accomplished without special means that are themselves not automatically accepted by all. Externally, it simply is the case that no philosophical program ever gains complete acceptance by all philosophers. As long as alternative ways of going about philosophy remain open, there can be no necessity or certainty about any one way of doing philosophy. Thus, finality cannot be achieved, because the discovery of another theory always remains an open possibility.

The question at issue now is the desirability of certainty and necessity as philosophical goals and the acceptability of anything else. What can our "negative way" tell us here? If a rejection of an argument for the existence of God cannot itself achieve universal acceptance, and if the epistemological grounds required remain under question and the whole purpose of rejecting a direct approach to God fails to achieve the necessity and certainty which prompted the rejection in the first place, then uncertainty results in any case.

Uncertainty simply seems to be our lot, even when we eliminate the consideration of God as a cause of philosophical uncertainty. This being the case, there is no really good reason to reject a view of God philosophically due to the uncertainty he

9

brings with him, since any method is basically subject to similar doubts in the long run. The objection to any concept of God on the basis of the epistemological uncertainty it produces leads us to see that certainty is not possible in any case, and a view of God must now be built upon uncertainty.

This is the first issue to be settled: What do we expect as a result of our philosophical analysis? If we are willing to accept nothing beyond probabilities—as Kant was not—then God as a philosophical object is not subject to any greater restrictions or difficulties than apply to every other philosophical enterprise. This does not force any philosopher to consider God who does not want to, but it does remove the restrictions against doing so on any supposed ground of winning a greater finality for our philosophical conclusions. Atheism calls into question the view of philosophy upon which the argument "against God" is based, and this opens up philosophy once again to its most fundamental question, i.e., what it is as a discipline and what it can claim to accomplish.

Considering God always forces us back to this basic issue. As we analyze any argument advocating technical atheism, we discover that it depends for its force on a certain view of philosophy, its methods and its goals. To call into question both the issue and the procedure itself—this has always been philosophy's peculiar distinction among the forms of inquiry. This explains the special fascination which the arguments for God's existence and denying God's existence have always held for philosophers. In the course of considering these, the question of philosophy itself is raised and answered, either implicitly or explicitly.

Where minor issues in philosophy are concerned, it is possible to enter into a discussion without raising directly the fundamental question of the nature of philosophical inquiry and its goals. Technical intricacies dominate the center of attention, and the discussion goes forward largely by pointing out some procedural oversight or logical inconsistency in the argument. On the other hand, even for those who share little in common with Anselm or who are opposed to Hume's conclusions, in each philosophical generation new proponents of Anselm's ontological argument and new objectors to Hume's conclusions arise.

10

Supposedly killed many times, by either flawless support or ir-refutable objection, these arguments and their proponents and opponents have a curiously continued vitality. Why? Because consciously or unconsciously this issue of God raises the ques-tion of philosophy's ultimate aim and procedure, even when the attention is apparently centered only on some particular aspect of proof or disproof.

God puts the question to philosophy about method I Cor 1-2

The question of God's existence keeps philosophy constantly conscious of itself and its nature, and it does this better than any other philosophical question, no matter how traditional. Do the arguments against God's existence do this any more clearly for us than the arguments which supposedly "prove" it? The answer is Yes. Why? Because, although the arguments for God's exis-tence equally involve and depend upon a particular view of philosophy's method and goal, these assumptions are not always so evident. They are seldom argued for directly and usually can only be inferred indirectly.

Anselm's ontological argument, for instance, changes in inter-pretation greatly depending on how his philosophical context is interpreted, but the argument itself has an apparent orientation forward, and not backward to consider philosophy's founda-tions. Deducing how Anselm uses philosophy is a rewarding task, but his argument itself does not require us to do this. On the other hand, Kant's *Critique* or Hume's *Dialogues* clearly define a method for philosophy. Here we see that objections to the proofs for God arise clearly as by-products in the develop-ment of that particular view of philosophy, as if they were a test for the validity of that way of doing philosophy itself. You under-stand why Hume rejects certain proofs for God when you under-stand his suggestion that philosophy should base itself on immediate perception combined with custom, for example. Ac-cepting or rejecting what Hume concludes about God is almost as simple as agreeing or disagreeing with his proposals for the basis of philosophy itself (i.e., custom, human nature, and im-mediate sense impressions).

Yet, illuminating as negative arguments may be about the particular view of philosophy upon which they are based, the experiences and problems that lead to the denial in the first place

11

are even more important. Men may toy casually with some positive theory, but negative arguments always seem to be brought forth by hard experience. The denial is usually a means of protection against some destructive power. The forces that destroy life and seem evil in their intent are, of course, the great sources of negativity. When you feel the impact of brutal destruction or experience an overwhelming sense of meaninglessness and futility, the mind is often compelled either to construct arguments denying God's existence or to attack those that support it. If we experience the negativity of evil, God's existence in any normal positive sense appears as a threat which must be opposed, because it is too disturbing emotionally to feel the reality of evil and at the same time believe in a simply good God. "The Devil," whenever he is seen, causes negative forces to be set into play.

If such brutal destruction as men have witnessed exists, there cannot be a God of the serene type often imagined by some overly pious devotees. Men have tasted emptiness and been struck by the force of negativity, therefore God must be denied. This is our immediate reaction when we feel the force of evil, and yet a less impulsive course is also possible. That is, in line with the violence encountered, we may ask what kind of God could still be compatible with the destruction experienced? Granted that there is no event which God could not have excluded from the world if he had so willed, what does the forceful presence of negativity tell us about a God who would create a world in which such things are even possible? The encounter with the world's violence often leads to a denial of God, and he is sometimes denied with a force almost equal to the destructiveness encountered. Would it not be possible to redirect such a negative impulse and make this force create a new and positive view of God, if it could be deduced from the very fact of such violence and negativity?

In that sense, the best empirical evidence for God's existence turns out to be what originally drove us to deny it. Ironically, this is often more real and concrete than the supposed positive evidence for a God. Could "the Devil" be the basis upon which a theory of God is constructed, there might be much more solid

12

ground in experience than for many abstract arguments purportedly based on God himself. What should our concept of God be like if evil is so real and powerful? This is the fundamental question. Any argument away from God's existence may also lead to it, by use of the negative evidence as a basis upon which to construct a theory of God that can accept into itself the negative argument without self-destruction.

The slaughter of the Jews in modern Germany has had a traumatic effect; it leads men either toward God or away from him. It leads Sartre away in *The Condemned of Altona*. Can this procedure be reversed? What kind of God can we construct who might allow such potential brutal destruction to exist in a world when he could have ruled it out? Of course, we may not succeed in forming such a picture of God, but if we do, it would certainly be a more real and powerful concept because of its capacity to accept such destruction into its nature. Or, if like Nietzsche one sees religion as restricting man's powers for advancement, then, rather than announcing God's death as Nietzsche does, this might incite men to revolt to form a new concept of a more powerful God. This is a struggle certainly more dramatic and terrifying than emancipation from a dead God. What kind of real God would allow religion and his own worship to enslave men at times? Are there avenues for protest against such a God which Nietzsche did not explore? To do battle may be much more exciting than to attend a funeral.

That road is more dangerous, and it is always uncertain from one moment to the next whether the outcome will be positive or negative, but this seems to be the religious road our age has chosen. God has seemed neither so attractive nor so powerful in our day as the negative forces we have symbolized as "the Devil." If this merely indicates that God is more hidden in his ways, that is not a solution, but rather the start of an attempt to uncover what his ways are. An overt Devil, if properly interrogated, may be of more help here than a silent God.

There are many possible concepts of God, and it is hard to decide among them on any concrete grounds. Devils are more real, and surely there are as many possible shapes of the Devil as there are possible views of God. Goodness has usually been

13

assumed as the road to God. How fascinating, if in our time evil should prove a better avenue to the consideration of God's existence than any attempt at a direct approach to God could ever be. Tame Gods, accept goodness easily, and no risk is involved for man. To accept evil into himself, however, requires a powerful God and also one with whom it is more dangerous for man to deal. Here lies the forceful source of atheism. Yet the hope of a new discovery seems worth any possible loss we risk in fully exploring its origins.

CHAPTER II

A God in Hiding

If evil occasionally bursts upon the public scene with all-too-evident destructive results, God unfortunately is not so obvious. It is perhaps God's silence and hiddenness that have most often led to atheism, both in technical argument and in private anguish. This does not mean that all men at all times have found God silent and hidden. Individuals often claim to have heard God clearly, but only rarely does this seem to possess a universal validity. All confidence in hearing God is confined to the particular person or the immediate group addressed. Religions, of course, are frequently organized around some appearance or speaking of God, as are Judaism and Christianity. Here, in the sacred literature and in the work of the community of believers, God's hiddenness and silence are broken. We cannot examine these claims in detail, but valid as the experience of God's presence may seem to the believer, it has seldom carried much weight in technical argument outside the community.

Why is that? The answer seems as simple as the fact that evil can be felt and seen by all, whereas the words in which the believer puts his trust as being from God are not so easily known to be divine. Strangely enough, we can unite a majority of men against what is evil, even if there is no corresponding unity of believers about the exact nature of their Gods. Faced with agreement about obvious evil, we find no similar unity as to God or his actions to balance it. Any individual within a religious tradition may work out a theology for himself, or a given tradition

15

may devise means for unifying its belief. Still, it is the case that the traditions themselves are not united; the destructive forces loose in the world do not have any divine opponent who is equally visible.

If atheism often stems from God's invisibility and his silence in the face of "the Devil," any useful theism must begin by accounting for God's silence and his failure to appear openly. Any God could have designed a world in which his presence would be unavoidably obvious. That he did not choose such a world or such an open expression for himself ought to tell us a great deal about his nature. If God's hiddenness leads to atheism, theism must test its validity by its ability to account for God's silence as opposed to evil's openness.

To begin with, it is interesting to note that there is a parallel problem where men are concerned. Although it constantly breaks out into the open, one reason evil is not always apparent is that men's real natures are all too often also hidden. Evil conceals itself, whenever possible, under a good surface; it works its way without arousing public opposition if it can. Thus a man's true nature is often hidden, and one must begin by trying to discover what is beneath the surface of both the words and the appearance of any person. Often we must go through this even with ourselves; the need for such discovery is not restricted only to other selves. Freud and the problem of the unconscious are but one example of this. If we must spend our lives trying to decipher the reality behind a man's words and actions, at least we see that God's nature is not the only one requiring indirect inference. Man too is mysterious.

The nature of neither God nor man is evident. Both must be discovered and made plain, or declared not to be different from what is seen. "Behaviorism" as a theory does for man what atheism does for God. If behaviorism were true, men would only be what they appear to be. If this were so, it would be the easiest solution, but it does not seem to do justice to the complexity of man or to the problem of trying to understand a man's true intent. Atheism declares that there is nothing hidden behind the events apparent in the world. If so, the prominence of evil, plus the absence of an overtly active God, supports atheism. If in the

16

case of man we recognize that the most important qualities are not always seen, and if we prize above all the writer who is able to reveal a man's nature through the medium of words, it does not seem quite so unlikely that God might exist and his nature still remain hidden beneath the surface of things.

If we are not simply what our external appearance indicates, then neither does God need to speak out directly. This is not to say that some actions of a man do not in fact reveal his nature, but it is interesting that it is more often an individual's actions than his words that do this. Some words reveal, but obviously not all words are to be trusted as a true indication. Our problem is to find a criterion to distinguish the true word from the false. That prized quality we attach to some very few words among all that are uttered.

Even if we use all the phenomena of the world as a base, God can never be seen directly from them. It is not an easy matter to discover what experiences do in fact reveal God's existence, and no one can be forced to recognize them, just as no one can be forced to believe that a man is false if he utters true words. Thus we differ over men, since their surfaces may always be taken for what they appear to be and as true in themselves. Whether the subject is God or man, to argue that something other than the appearance is true is always the most difficult case, and the odds are against accepting it. A man's nature is often revealed only after his death. Perhaps it is not a bad thing that the death of God has been proclaimed, since now we can determine whether the concept we have held hitherto is true or not.

If men can neither be judged by their exterior nor have all their words accepted, perhaps it is not so strange that God does not speak out directly very often. In such a situation we are left free to form our concept of God in a variety of ways. One word from God would put an end to this variety and bring a unity of concepts out of plurality. The fact that variety in conceptualization remains should in itself tell us a great deal about God, but this point will be developed more fully later. Since he could have made himself overt and authorized a single concept of his nature, it must be that he did not wish to do so. If God always spoke

17

directly, it would remove our uncertainty, but it would also remove our freedom. Much greater uncertainty is involved if God remains silent, but this alone does not solve the problem, since freedom and variety could have been left open to us without either such a baffling world as we have or the extent of violent destruction that prevails in it. Obviously we are dealing with a God who felt perfectly capable of electing a more destructive world than was necessary in order to achieve his purpose.

Take cancer as a small example. If medical men succeed in discovering a cure for this killer as they have for other dread diseases, it will come only after centuries, after uncountable deaths and unspeakable suffering. God might easily have eliminated this in the beginning by building in the same methods which science may yet discover. He could have incorporated them in the original model at creation. Let us say that he did not wish to do it this way. Still, a few words uttered earlier in the process could have speeded man's discovery of a cure. In the face of this question we hear only silence. On the other side, in God's defense it can be said that at least a cure was not ruled out and that relief may yet be found. Clearly we are dealing with a God who could have caused or speeded the relief of human suffering and did not choose to do so. He could have, or else the men who laboriously work out these remedies are more intelligent than he. This fact is probably the strongest impulse toward atheism and the greatest destroyer of theistic arguments today; and yet, if it is turned around, what kind of God could it lead to?

First of all, we know that God is never immediately present in any absolutely confirming manner. He always remains at least somewhat hidden, and it is true that whatever is not said directly is always capable of being denied. This being the case, no definitive argument for God's existence can ever be established; but, on the other hand, no argument against a God who is so hidden can ever be concluded either. We are left in an in-between state, a no-man's-land. Since God has not elected to be obvious, his existence and his nature are always subject to doubt. No man can be forced to believe, but the way is also open for any man to read the indirect evidence and to form a conception of God, although

18

[handwritten marginal notes at top: Boy meets girl — never married — reveals — yet white heart ... that close! — college - but dropped out — good job, - in research — a new area exposed - opens an area of mystery. — a parable however is closer, reveals to ... nature of God. As one who in revealing, hides himself.]

A GOD IN HIDING

this must be one which can account for his hiddenness and his decision against an overt appearance. *A hidden God lends support to atheism, since only an apparent God could put an end to disbelief.* Such a situation requires interpretation, and thus it is always open to debate. Views may, of course, be put forth, but not all of them can be adequate, since no concept can reign clearly supreme under such conditions.

This is our situation with regard to God, and it is also the theme of existence. We are always so near and yet so far. If either the true nature of a man or the existence of God were discovered, nothing could be closer to us. Whenever in our relations with men we think we have discovered their true nature through surface words and actions, then distance is overcome and the nearness of association which we seek can be experienced at last. When men feel that they have discerned God through his silent surface, they often report it as mystical union, which is the closest of all possible relationships. Yet such rapport is difficult to achieve with man or God, and mystics report their inability to sustain such union beyond a brief time. Relations between men are also subject to constant change, even when a momentary penetration to the inner man has been experienced. Most men tend to react against it. They withdraw behind a surface cover in the fear that such exposure may restrict their freedom, which it does. We continually seek to uncover the inner man, and some men seek the hidden God; but we constantly feel so near and yet so far from achieving this.

We feel near because we think it possible to discern the inner nature beneath the surface, and yet far because we know that such insight is both impossible to sustain for very long and also exceedingly difficult to capture precisely in words. If the chief ground of atheism lies in the hidden nature of God, at least it is clear that such is also the theme of our whole existence among men. Our relationship to God is thus not essentially on a very different plane, except that in man's case at least we are confronted by the overt and concrete actions of an embodied individual. We have trouble discovering and explaining in words what the inner man is, but with God we do not even have much tangible area to focus on. To overcome this hid-

19

Faith requires willingness to go beneath the obvious.

denness is perhaps the world's hardest problem.

Do those who demand openness in man's nature also tend toward atheism because God is hidden? It would seem so. A willingness to struggle for a revealing glance into a man's inner nature and the rejection of the simple substitute of accepting his outer nature and words as being true—this seems to be coupled with at least a willingness to consider that God might exist and still be hidden from our sight. Then all those who demand disclosure as an indispensable condition for belief force themselves toward atheism, since such complete openness of God is not available to us, or it would have been made plain from the beginning.

Can we accept a situation of permanent hiddenness, one which allows only difficult and brief disclosures? If not, atheism is the only alternative, and some of the most intriguing and baffling sides of man will also be lost. Life is simpler when it is identified with its surface, but it is also less exciting, less dangerous, and perhaps less creative. Still, we have the responsibility to offer an account of why God might have chosen to conceal himself when he need not have done so. In order to do this we must be prepared to accept a much more difficult and less serene concept of God. An easy, friendly God would have no reason to hide himself.

What kind of God would conceal himself in creating a world and then wrap man's nature in a puzzle when he did not have to? The least we can do is to try to frame a concept of God that fits what is evident—and what is evident is just that he is, if he exists, usually concealed. If God had *intended* to be open but somehow remained obscure, that would involve stupidity in designing a man so obtuse that he could not see what was evident. Or else it would indicate a clumsy self-presentation on the part of God—a picture so sorry that we would (like Hume) prefer none at all.

Let us give God credit and assume that the situation we perceive is exactly as he intended it. He could easily have instituted a different design if he had cared to. If we begin with the fact that he is not evident but instead concealed himself in creating our world, what kind of respectable God can we argue

20

for, as intending things to be exactly that way?

First of all, he must be a God who is not dependent upon men in order to exercise sufficient control to accomplish his purposes. If he were man-dependent, he would seem to have chosen a very risky path in concealing himself. Even when instructions are clear and open and definite, men have enough trouble in following them. If God depends upon us to accomplish his purpose, the least he could do to insure the cooperation necessary to him would be to make the instructions plain. It would be a foolish and somehow rather precarious God who did not at least do what he could to issue clear instructions, if he needs our help; let us not assume a foolish God as long as we can find a more intelligent one to explain things.

If God is not dependent upon us for cooperation, he risks nothing of his purpose in remaining hidden, for he must be able to accomplish it without making himself public. Furthermore, he must be a God who is not concerned to make his intentions continually obvious. He does not feel the need to explain himself to man. Self-justification is, as Kierkegaard points out, an impulse of youth. Nor is it imperative that the balance always appear in his favor whenever a subtotal is struck. It would be easy to make men believe in him if he did operate in this way, so he must be above anxious concern over whether men acknowledge his presence and his intent at any given moment. If he wanted his situation to be different, he certainly selected the poorest possible means to ensure a clear relationship between God and man.

Every empirical fact or action in the world must be capable of telling us something, since every feature could easily have been different. That is, each event informs us that it was consciously chosen against its alternatives, since we now assume a God who selected a less obvious relationship than possible. Ours is not at all the best possible world, as all-too-human Leibnitz thought; it is merely the one which God willed as capable of being a vehicle for his purpose. Next we must ask what his purpose might be in concealing himself, and in revealing his nature as much in the possibility and existence of evil as in good?

He is, we conclude, not dependent on us for cooperation, and

21

thus cannot have been intent upon creating an atmosphere in which men would naturally acknowledge his presence or even be able to see at any given moment that his purpose would indeed be accomplished. The present balance does not give us a clue to the end. That is, it does not if the outcome is to be other than the mixed picture of victory and destruction currently in evidence. Such a God must be powerful enough to play a dangerous game, for by concealing his intentions he loses powerful human allies whom he might easily have had on his side if only he had made this clear. He invites men to curse him in the circumstances which he has created, and gives no easy evidence of his presence or his intent to accomplish anything in the world other than what in fact now can be seen by all.

He must, then, prefer indirection to direct confrontation. Even if Moses is right and man cannot see God and live, there are still many more explicit ways of communication than the one which he seems to have chose. In fact, the difficulties present in his means of communication more often cause discussion and controversy than unity, and God might so easily have made what he wished to say more obvious than, say, the message of the New Testament is. Many read but few agree.

He is a God who rejected simple clarity. The British empiricists have been foiled by a God who will not cooperate with them and create the world along simple lines. Yet the frustration of a British empiricst is nothing when compared with the suffering of the innocent and the mangling of the bodies of those who are caught in the clash of powers. He must, then, be a God who does not faint at the sight of blood or lie awake because sufferers scream. This does not mean that he intends to do nothing about all this or that he is insensitive, but it certainly does mean that he has deliberately rejected a world in which such pain might have been either eliminated or reduced from the beginning. Clearly he does not intend to intervene very often to prevent needless suffering or to put an end to pain.

Man can accomplish improvement, of course. Thus, we are dealing with a God who did at least leave open the possibilities for advance, but we are not facing one who made the remedies at all easy to find or to administer. Aside from what his frame-

22

work allows men to accomplish, if he intends to make any corrections on his part, they are not easy to discern; and certainly they are, with perhaps relatively minor exceptions, all still to be accomplished. He must be a God who does not care much for uniformity of opinion. Men have been struggling to impose unalterable conclusions on each other for centuries, and they are no closer than ever to necessity and certainty on the crucial theoretical matters, although we still talk about achieving this goal. We are faced with a God who reversed the important and the unimportant. He designed a world in which the unimportant can be agreed upon and need not cause us trouble, although some men force trivia to do so. What is important seems not quite subject to an infinite variety of interpretations, but it is involved in at least a sufficient variety to keep us either constantly at odds or else talking at cross purposes.

Had he wanted one philosophy, one theology, or even one scientific theory, God could easily have worked out a theoretical structure accordingly. That such uncertainty has persisted for so many centuries is perhaps not so much our fault (as some philosophers have thought) as it is a testimony to the fact that God originally preferred variety to unity and a lack of finality to certitude. Since he ordered our world with that in mind, we should long ago have given up upbraiding each other for not settling theoretical issues once and for all. Instead we should ask: What kind of God we are dealing with who has preferred to place us in such an inconclusive position?

A God who hides cannot have one theology written about him or expect to be understood in one way. In order to put an end to variety of opinion, he would have to speak with one voice, which he has not heretofore done (not even via Peter's successors). This basic human uncertainty apparently does not concern him as much as it does us. After all, our anxiety in these matters arises from our awareness that we do not have unimpeachable answers available. On the other hand, if God correctly understands himself and the power of his word, he need not care about achieving a universality of theory. He can speak and act when he needs to and wants to. Only when the sufficiency of power is in doubt does an absolute agreement of opinion become an

23

item of concern as it does between nervous men.

God evidently can afford the luxury of not coercing others to adopt his views. Such a God must be rather relaxed where theory is concerned, since he is not as dependent on it as we are to accomplish our ends. Nor need such a God act at every time in the same way; if he did, his ultimate intentions would be evident in his previous acts. A God whose action is consistent with his hiddenness does not need to disclose himself to others—that human impulse which testifies to our inadequacies and leads us both to so much intimacy and to so much harm. It apparently does not upset him to be misunderstood, for he has as yet taken no sides in theological and philosophical debates.

This does not mean that those who claim to support him may not actually be doing so; it is only that their assistance is not crucial. Nor does this mean that those who claim to have seen God may not have done so in some sense, but only that he does not reveal himself very clearly or publicly and in a manner calculated to remove all confusion. Nor does this necessarily mean that he has not upon occasion intervened to heal suffering or to comfort the distressed; it is only that millions are rejected for the few who are chosen. The exceptions allowed are much less than even a compassionate human being might make. The score is not complete, of course, but so it stands after quite a few centuries of play.

It is not at all impossible, then, to construct a view of God consistent with the very arguments for atheism. It is not a very comfortable picture, and we might wish it were less harsh, but it does seem that a God can be found who is consistent with those factors which drive men to atheism. Although, as Plato discovered long ago, it is not at all necessary that we have completely clear knowledge in advance, it is still true that a rejection can only be made on the basis of some positive information. In this case the philosopher's job is still to bring to light the as yet unclear standards implicitly used as the basis for rejecting a God. Atheism in our day is not saying that we do not have a concept of God. What is being formed but is not yet fully expressed is just enough to make us reject a previous concept of God as not adequate. The as yet unseen

24

future concept still needs to be stated precisely.

If we examine the causes and the arguments for atheism and admit fully their power to lead us away from some one concept of God, and if we do reverse the negative impulse and attempt to construct a view of God built upon the factors which lead to his rejection—what then? Does any argument so constructed have universal and necessary power to convince us all? No, but any demand that it should have such universal validity itself rests on a view of the nature of argument and of human rationality which needs critical examination. For what makes us suppose that any argument in philosophy ought to carry universality? Such a view involves a whole theory of the nature and function of philosophy, and it needs prior analysis if any discussion of God is to be meaningful. For if philosophical theory and method are not such as to provide a firm and unalterable conviction in every case, then an argument for God—provided it is possible —suffers no more than any other philosophical theory if it lacks universality and necessity.

Yet even on such a view of philosophical statements, i.e., as not being made of such rigid stuff as to achieve unalterability, what happens to the person who listens openly to a description of God constructed on the basis of the arguments for atheism? Is his mind led to apprehend such a God of atheism or not? It is not—that is, if he does not require an explanation for why the frame of the world is shaped in this way and not in another possible form. Naturalism is always a tenable position, and anyone who wishes to adopt it cannot be moved from it. If you want simply to accept the structure as you find it, and if you do not consider our world's form as merely one possibility among others, you are not required to give an account of why the selection process came out the way it did. To do that means to build a theory of God's nature which includes the rationale governing his decisions. This involves not only an account of the process of development but a theory accounting for the selection of the original elements.

There are those who do seek a way to explain how our world came to have its particular shape from among all its possible forms, but an evolutionary process of selection does not explain

Exactly

this. It only outlines the means for developing the potentials once the initial framework has been fixed; it does not tell us how this process and its particular materials happened to be chosen over others. A God constructed from the arguments which tend to reject his existence does have the peculiar virtue of being able to answer the question of why we have this particular form of a world rather than some other comprised of different elements. For the factors which lead to atheism are most often those features of the world which one objects to and would like to have removed, and these harsh features are incompatible with a simple Platonic notion of an all-good God. However, a concept of God built precisely to account for these objectionable facts yeilds an explanation of why these features were purposefully selected for inclusion in our world while some others were not, and it has that advantage.

To the extent that we are successful in constructing a view of God based on the sources of atheism, we answer precisely the basic question of modern metaphysics: "Why is the world formed in this way and not in another?" To be sure, we need a God who is capable of explaining himself. Otherwise we have not reached the end of the argument or really explained the choice of the world's form. In accounting for how the mechanisms of the world were selected when they might have been quite different, if you build a picture of God capable of accounting for his own nature and his choice of the world's particular form, you may actually have an argument capable of leading first to atheism and then back again away from it.

From examining the forces of atheism we learn how to put and how not to put the question of God's existence. Our first consideration must always be: Is this a proper question to ask about God? In this way we discover what questions, if they are not reformulated, are bound to lead to atheism. Our problem, thus, becomes one of seeing how to reformulate the question so that it may lead, by moving in the opposite direction, to a new and more adequate concept of God. Take for example the chief problem, i.e., evil in the form of undeserved suffering on the part of the innocent. If you have a concept of God which cannot be reconciled with undeserved suffering, of course such an opposi-

26

Then we are setting up the construal. Let the evidence speak itself

tion will lead to atheism. We should not begin with a concept of God and then hold to it firmly in an unmodified form in order to determine whether the world is or is not compatible with it. Rather, beginning with a concept of God held only tentatively, if we learn that, say, undeserved suffering is incompatible with it, the impulse toward atheism should then refashion the concept of God itself. We ask: What altered concept of God could be compatible with the undeserved suffering actually present in the world?

When a concept of God tends to be rejected, it is much better to let it go. However, if we try to erect upon the very evidence that rejected it a more adequate concept, a certain risk is involved. In surrendering an old concept rather than trying to patch it up, we may only lose what we had and not gain anything new in its place. Yet out of such a void—one into which we are propelled by atheism—a new concept may be formed, and the risk seems worth the possible loss.

It is interesting to note that the idea that such a shift in concepts is necessary fits into our basic premise of a hidden God. It is hard enough to tie down what is obvious to some one particular conceptualization, even if in fact this is ultimately either possible or desirable. In the case of a hidden God, however, the indirection necessary in order to deal with him seems to give rise to a constant natural tendency toward atheism. Occasionally we have a fruitful and venturesome rebellion that results in a revised and more adequate concept of God. A certain technical formulation of the divine nature may seem adequate at a certain time, but, given a hidden God who cannot be equated, identified, or compared with any single idea, even such a temporarily adequate concept must be redone from time to time in order to retain its power—remolded by the constant problem of atheism.

There are many ways to live but only one way to die, that is by ceasing to live. There are good reasons why the existentialist writers have focused on the phenomenon of death. Sartre has tried to explain that this emphasis does not arise from an excessive morbidity but actually from an effort to find a meaning and a direction for life from the impact of its negative threat. This

27

is much like our attempt to construct a theory of God's nature from a study of the Devil. One hundred per cent agreement is seldom possible, and yet more men do recognize that cutting off a man's life is an evil than could ever agree on a single right way to live. For this reason we cannot write as easily about what is good as we can about what is evil, i.e., wantonly destructive. This is of course a relative matter, and even about the evils of the world there is some disagreement. It is just that, in their blatant life-denying form, we seem more able to unite against what is to be avoided and opposed as an evil threat than to agree to promote some individual good.

Many philosophical views have tried to construct theories of the good, with varying degrees of success. If good could be defined simply as happiness, as some have attempted to do, it might not be so hard to agree upon. Simple as it would be if adopted, this definition has never been able to gain complete acceptance. However, some will even claim that to die for a good cause is a good thing. If this were not possible, wars and self-sacrifice would have ceased long ago. We do differ as to whether sacrifice of life is ever good, but the thing to be noted is that we seldom if ever call the death itself a good thing.

If release from life or suicide is ever said to be good, again it is the suffering escaped from or the tortures avoided which make such a death good and not the loss of life itself. Usually death is called a good thing when there is already at least a half-death involved. Actually it is the escape from other forces which have already thwarted life that is the good rather than the death itself. Could life really be lived, then death would never be preferable. Men "die" partially in many ways. Thus, if one has ceased to live either spiritually or morally, death may be good as a release from an already partial death, but not as opposed to the full exertion of one's power. To live is to be able to exert power. Evil always means the blocking or cutting down of a person's ability to exercise his power, and we have symbolized this real force in the personified concept of the Devil.

All exercise of power is not good, and occasionally we kill justifiably either because someone has abused the use of power or because we want to prevent power from being abused. In these

28

cases we destroy life or power and do not call it evil. Why not? Usually this is when power runs amuck and either threatens or already has destroyed the life of others. Murder may accomplish certain ends. When it does, then we may agree or disagree as to whether the ends justified the destruction of life, but we never call the murder itself a good thing. We are most horrified whenever we face the wanton destruction of a life filled with meaning or purpose, and this indicates that it is the *goal* of the killing that we may *sometimes* call good, but seldom if ever the destruction of life itself. We may gloss over an evil which has a good motive, but, when the destruction is without purpose, the confusion of good and evil clears up, and we can see such sudden death as in itself a simple evil.

Evils, of course, are of many kinds, and the most important distinction has always been between those of natural and of human origin. When natural disasters strike, we consider the destruction of life involved to be an evil. Interestingly enough, we are united on this more often than not, since the supposedly good intentions of some moral evil clouds the issue of the loss of life involved as being clearly an evil. That is why war is always a controversial issue, since some will point to its asserted good purposes while those who oppose it point to the loss of life. The opponents of war always have the clearer case, since loss of life is always an evil. On the other hand, the purposes accomplished by war are sometimes good and sometimes not, or at best they are mixed or questionable.

However, where God is concerned this distinction between natural and moral evil breaks down, and as far as the problem of theodicy is concerned (i.e., God's involvement with the world and his intent), natural evil is almost more a problem than moral evil. God is held responsible for moral evil in the sense that he created a world in which such human actions are possible, whereas he might have created a world in which human evil was eliminated or at least lessened. Except on a totally deterministic view, man bears some of the responsibility for moral evil; but, as to the evils in nature, it is God alone who is held responsible for the kind of world in which they exert their destructive power.

This has not always been the case. An earlier metaphysical

29

view accepted our world as being without alternative, or at least considered God's selection of this world as necessary. This relieved God of some responsibility, although only at the price of binding him by a form of necessity. A free God is also a more responsible God, but he bears the guilt of the natural evil that is inflicted on man which need not have been. However, the problem of theodicy, as intensified under a theory of freedom, is not the issue here. Rather our concern is whether, from a study of evil of all types, a view of God's nature can be found which is adequate to include within it the forces of evil. "The Devil" is not a misleading name for the coalescence of the forces of destruction. Since we are forced to deal with a hidden God, we must try to consider him from the standpoint of the Devil. Thus, how evil is described is crucial to how God will be thought of.

CHAPTER III

Some Gods Are Easier to Find

If we engage in a little comparative study of possible concepts of God, one of the first things we note is that some Gods are easier to find than others. At first it might seem that the easier a God is to find the better, but atheism is instructive here and teaches us more than this. Since God is not obviously present in the world, a concept of God can never be fully confirmed no matter how clear it may seem in itself. Given the complexities and the difficulties in life, the more obvious the God the more the concept will also run into difficulties, since the world contains many problems which any durable concept of God must be able to cope with. Thus, the less easy it is to find, the more the concept is likely to be adequate to a world whose procedures also are not obvious. This is a mixed blessing, since the less obvious concepts of God are not so easily rejected, and yet they are also increasingly difficult to accept. The simpler a God is to find, the easier he is to reject. The harder he is to find, the more difficult he is to reject definitively, but the concept is also more difficult for us to confirm and maintain belief in.

What we learn from this is an interesting fact: There are as many arguments for—and against—God as there are concepts of God. We might find the situation easier to deal with if there were only a single agreed concept of God, but in no theoretical realm (certainly not in the physical sciences) does our task seem destined to be so simple. Faced with such conceptual complexity, it quickly becomes apparent that our problem is neither to reject

31

nor to accept some single offered concept, although often that is a necessary starting point. We must begin by sorting out the various concepts along a spectrum and then decide in which direction we wish to go in search of the most likely. With as many arguments as there are types of God, it is clear that a God who is too easy to find actually oversimplifies the complex conceptual problem which we face when we try to find—or to reject—God.

If it is true that there are as many arguments for—or against—God as there are types of concepts, we cannot expect to settle this issue once and for all. For no sooner do we establish—or deny—one concept than another springs up in its place. Not every concept is equally tenable, and some have achieved a classical status as highly possible, but our work in considering Gods can never be done as long as any concepts remain unexplored. We have reason to suspect that these are at least nearly infinite in variety. Yet we are not left in a state of complete chaos, since certain interesting features of this situation emerge which are instructive in themselves. We have already noted that a God who is too obvious seems inappropriate to such a complex situation, and that certain concepts (e.g., the Unmoved Mover) establish themselves as classical alternatives. These facts give some stability and a fixed point of reference to this shifting theological scene.

In approaching this arena from the problem of atheism, however, the most noticeable feature is that the weight pro and con is not evenly distributed. If it were so, then our situation would probably be worse, since we would remain motionless. But Kant is wrong, ours is not such a simple situation as to have arguments of equal weight on both sides. Some theists have hoped and sought to prove that the balance of power is in favor of some one concept of God, but unfortunately for the theologians the situation is worse than that. Atheism always has a slight balance in its favor. Unhappy as this seems, at least it does us the service of warning that any argument for God faces an uphill battle, and that it will have a natural tendency to lose its forcefulness and to slip back toward atheism.

Since every defect in our world seems to demand an explanation from theology, the issue over God has a negative slant at the outset. This is particularly true if you want to argue for a deity with good intentions, since the good features of the world can be accepted just as they are, while the evils and horrors seem to demand more explanation. This requires the construction of an intricate theoretical framework, and there is no way to force a man to go to all that trouble if he does not want to. Thus, it is more difficult to believe in a God than to accept nature for just what it is. The mystery really is why so many have ever come to believe in any concept of God at all in the face of such heavy odds.

This situation of imbalance, however, offers certain advantages to God in his race against atheism, since simple stupidity can be only a partial explanation of belief. Perhaps atheism itself accounts for the fact that there are those who have come to believe in a nonobvious God. That is, the tendency in nature towards atheism, plus the awareness that a simple answer does not seem appropriate to a nonobvious world—perhaps this drift in itself has set up a reaction that jars men into discovering how they ought to approach God conceptually.

Since it is not easy if we do think about God, something must drive us to, and keep us at, this difficult and often unpleasant task. If the destruction and the terror which have been set loose in the world often seem to deny God, the appalling presence of this violence may also force us to think about God in more profound ways than we might otherwise attain if we were left to float on the pleasant surface of life. The same forces that make men oppose God are also among the strongest powers operating to make us reach a more profound and complex theological view than we would otherwise need to do. An easy view of a pleasant God might be adequate if atheism were not so strong and so solidly rooted.

What this may tell us is that the waves of atheism and the pronouncements of God's death which we have witnessed in our time simply testify to the superficiality of our thinking about God—or perhaps to the fact that we have forgotten how to think about God at all. Simple Gods die easily; pleasant Gods are also pleasantly weak and submit to denial without a struggle. Each

33

new day demands a God sufficiently powerful to withstand the storms of that time. Just as anyone who experiences conversion, whether religious or psychic, must first touch the very lowest point that borders on total disintegration before he can move upward, so the force of an argument which can kill a God may also build up a new concept after it has destroyed the old one. The iconoclasm of our recent past may be an absolutely necessary step, since only destruction can clear the scene of the now forceless concepts of God. Our thinking may reach a more profound level in the process of sinking beneath once solid ground.

If accepting a God is always less obvious than taking Nature as self-explanatory, and if thinking about God requires us to open ourselves to the blasts of the forces which perpetually lead to atheism, such a game is surely lost as often as it is won. It is a wonder that so many play it, and it is even more startling that God emerges with as many followers as he does. It does not seem to be in man's nature to accept a more difficult explanation when a simpler one is available or to follow a more dangerous and upsetting path when more secure ways are known. What can explain man's action here?

First of all, just as in the world of commerce, not everyone is either ambitious or energetic enough to set out on a difficult course. It is always the creative few who are willing to gamble on high stakes and to pit their skill against precarious paths. The rewards of success—in business and in theology—are extremely high. Thus, in a vital society a gifted minority can often be found who will venture either in scientific theory or in thought about God. Yet that will lead only a very few to any new view of God, and as a matter of fact many who do not pit their skill against the world's forces also come to believe in a God. Perhaps men sense that the world and its structure are not at all easy to explain. A simple answer is easy; it just has no holding power. Since life is as difficult as it is, an obvious answer is attractive but not profound. Answers are not found without the pain of plunging beneath the obvious surface. Thus, God has some forces on his side, too.

If defining and believing in God is subject to so many difficulties, and if the believer cannot have his belief without some

34

mental anguish, the fact that so many do accept God indicates that complex answers can be forged and perhaps are more satisfying than simple ones. At times we try to make simple answers do, since it would be so much easier if they were accepted. Uncomplex answers are our only hope for achieving universality of opinion. As soon as they are rejected and more complicated and tortuous explorations attempted, we know that any solution proposed will at the same time be more realistic about the hidden sides of the world—but also more controversial.

Those who feel compelled to deny God also feel forced to argue for their denial, and those who reach a level of insight into God often shrink from any attempt to express it in conceptual forms. If God were an issue easily decided, the atheist could save his arguments and his bitter denials, since anyone with intelligence would silently come to the same conclusion. The obvious does not need expression. If thinking about God did not require the mental counterpart of physical suffering, those who achieve some insight would happily state their conclusion in simple terms. Only the most talented will risk reducing their views to print, and a surge of emotion always surrounds this issue. Perhaps the very difficulty of this situation explains the mystery of why so many do accept God and cannot accept either an obvious naturalism or a simple atheism.

What are the factors which combine here to make the problem of God so difficult? The answers are as many and as varied as the imperfections men find in the world, but the issue is concentrated in two words: destruction and violence. Sartre in his *The Devil and the Good Lord* portrays the sadistic sides of personified destruction,* and in the face of this he gives some very weak answers, which completely lack a force equivalent to the negative powers portrayed. No wonder he is an atheist. Once upon a time we did not understand how many options we actually have to the world we see around us; we thought its structure had to be as we find it. Now we know that it all did not have to be this way.** It certainly seems that, were God not a God of

*Jean-Paul Sartre, *The Devil and the Good Lord*, Kitty Black, trans. (New York: Vintage Books, 1960).

**For an expansion on this theme of the change in our situation regarding evil and the way in which we now see the world as not necessary, see my *God, Why*

35

violence, he would not have selected such a destructive world as ours. Violence is under control within his nature, although it is not always so for us. Nevertheless, this tendency to destruction must be a very strong side to God's nature too.

God might have created a peaceful and pastoral order. Of course, our world is like that at times and upon occasion, but it can also erupt and destroy. Sartre wants to find an answer for sadistic destruction, and a God who is completely unlike this cannot give a reply of sufficient force. In line with the freedom we feel, we do not want a God who designs every action, but we do need a God who selects both the type and the limits of our order, i.e., an order within which violence is possible when it might not have been permitted. Both God and man need more freedom; a man needs to be free from divine individual determination, and we must learn to think of God as free and strong enough to choose the order he wills. A God who intends only good—in some simple sense—cannot account for widespread destruction. Only one who is powerful enough to choose a mixed order deliberately can provide the strong answer required here.

Even if God chose a world with the degree of violence and destruction which we find, this does not mean it is a good thing to accept it without protest or that we cannot oppose it or improve it. What this does mean is that we have a God capable of deliberate destruction and of making us face overwhelming odds upon occasion. Attributing goodness to him is not impossible, but certainly it is not a simple matter. Any divine goodness must have hidden features, and it can only be a very complex kind of goodness. If one has a simple notion of goodness, the forces in nature make it difficult to hold on to God when that uncomplicated goodness proves no longer adequate.

We exist in an order in which violence and destruction are not sufficient to tear the order itself into shreds and cause it to fall apart. Yet neither is violence present on a scale such that its effects are merely minor inconveniences. The forces we face can kill and destroy and break loose on a mass scale, although it is

---

Did You Do That? (Philadelphia: Westminster Press, 1970).

also possible to contain them and to have eras of fruitful tranquillity. Goodness in this light takes on a new meaning and an added complexity. Form and order and balance, when they are achieved, are not arrived at automatically but only with conscious effort and against powers which would deny them life if they could. When goodness comes too easily, it is not likely to survive very long. What is produced in the face of obstacles commands our attention and respect. A good God would not just act, but he might mold powerful forces in spite of all threats against them.

We sometimes associate goodness with economy, but clearly that is too simple where God is concerned. Economically speaking, he has produced a rather wasteful order. In order to produce some good life, much has been spent to no good purpose. A world might have been designed in which each child was formed perfectly and born to live out his life span. Instead, a great deal is lost in the process of producing some useful life, and the waste in this process causes considerable pain. Some of this might have been eliminated in a more neatly planned system. Monsters are rather useless creatures and give only grief to their parents. True, some handsome things are born and develop, but our world need not have been as wasteful as it is in order to be able to achieve this end. The argument that we need a degree of contrast in order to appreciate the good is valid only up to a point, for we could still appreciate the beauties we have if a little less suffering and waste surrounded them.

Why was this unnecessarily wasteful order selected by God? If the same ends could have been achieved by less destructive and wasteful means, it would seem that he rejected the use of an easier path. His goodness must be such that it does not have to express itself by the easiest and simplest means, in spite of the fact that the rationalist philosophers think in this way. God sacrifices more than he needs, to produce so little beauty, and he sends us down a harder road than it is necessary to follow in order to achieve our ends or to appreciate beauty. We could achieve understanding with less violence and hardship. We seem to labor under unnecessary burdens, particularly when they are placed upon those who break under them. We could come to feel what suffering is like without being driven to insanity. Our concept of goodness in God, then, has to be revised to allow for a willful inclusion of insanity when he might have designed an all-sane world.

To understand goodness in God as being compatible with both a personal and a public irrationality which he might have eliminated—this is not a simple concept to form. A God like this is not easy but rather hard to find. He must be able to sustain the weight of the argument against him, to accept the blame for the evil which he might easily have eliminated, and above all, to be strong enough in constitution to witness more crushing evil than we are capable of taking in all at once or would care to. Evil is more deeply felt than pleasure and more difficult to ignore. One can smile and casually pass by those engaged in the pleasures of life. One may praise God for them, but there is nothing about pleasure that requires us to do so. The witnessing of destructive evil, on the other hand, is harder to ignore, although some manage to do so, and it is more likely to bring a denunciation of God than good is likely to bring praise. Strange that God should both allow evil such wanton destructive power and permit it to weigh more heavily than good.

Good leads to a God that seems to know no evil, and this does not really help at all to explain the world as we know it. Evil at first seems to lead away from God, but could we discover a God strong enough to be hidden behind evil, that which explains evil might account for good also. Ludwig Feuerbach thought that God was merely man's wish in a corporeal form.* If we shape our idea of God only from the good in the world, this might be true. If we follow atheism and allow evil to reject a God of simple goodness, any idea of God we can construct from atheism's strongest incentive—i.e., destructive evil—cannot be made of man's wishes. Our wishes are dreams, and only a few malignant individuals dream of evil.

A God found in this manner is precisely what man does not dream romantic dreams about. In our Freudian dreams we see evil eliminated and our wishes fulfilled. Our wish is that every

*See Ludwig Feuerbach, *The Essence of Christianity*, George Eliot, trans. (New York: Harper Torchbooks, 1957), especially Chapter I.

38

obstacle in our way be removed, and the destructive forces which always threaten to tear down both ourselves and our projects are what we want to eliminate. A God who is discovered in examining evil, however, is one who willfully permits it when he might have omitted it. Thus, rather than God allowing us to escape from evil into the world of our dreams, if atheism leads to a God it will be to one who insists that we live with the world exactly as it was made, and not escape from it in dreaming.

Were God a God of goodness only he would have no reason to hide himself, as he seems to have done. Were he and his creation all good, God and men could be friends openly and neither would have anything to conceal. That all evil results from man's free act and that only man has a reason to hide himself —this is simply not true. Adam may be in the wrong in the Genesis story, but God must not be allowed to hide behind Adam's innocence. If evil is all man's fault, God should exist in openness, since man alone has done wrong and God would have no reason to hide. Whatever evil man has done and will yet do is hard to accept, but we can come to live with it. It is even harder to adjust to God's intentional design of this world; the tearing of flesh and the destruction of the innocent which he allows to go on within it are hard on the religious spirit. We are not rewarded according to our goodness or punished only if we are evil. Destruction when it comes rains down in democratic fashion killing good and bad alike. Pleasure is not forbidden to the wrongdoer. If God has hidden himself behind evil, it may be only there and not in simple goodness that he can be found.

The heart of darkness seems a strange place to look in our attempt to bring God out of hiding. Yet that is where the center of the problem of atheism lies. If we are in fact dealing with a hidden God, we must explain the most difficult and not merely the easiest facts. A Thomistic God who explains motion and purpose is fine, but disorder is more our problem than order. God as the source of all goodness is all right, but goodness itself does not demand much explanation. Evil does require an accounting, and its explanation is certainly not to be found on the surface, or we would have stopped worrying long ago. Evil leads naturally to atheism, so that any God uncovered here will start with

39

the strongest possible arguments. If the primary source of evil
turns out to be in God himself, uncovering these hidden origins
will also lead us to a God otherwise concealed. God has hidden
himself in evil, apparently, and he is to be discovered there or
not at all. The God of evil is very hard to find, but perhaps he
is the only God strong enough to withstand the natural tendency
toward atheism.

CHAPTER IV

The Odds Against God

One of the main factors contributing to the problem of atheism is the tendency we have to equate "good" with the sacred and "evil" with the profane. Sometimes, of course, it is the other way around, and those who stress the faults of organized religion find nothing good in the sacred and instead identify all that is good with the secular order. To do either is an oversimplification and also the source of much confusion. To understand why good and evil cannot be so simply divided along these lines is of course also to learn something important about an argument for God. That this is true is due to the fact that, in this day, any God must account for both good and evil on a positive basis and not simply by negation as Augustine would prefer. To do this requires a new understanding of good and evil, and this can only be one which separates it along no simple line of sacred and profane.

If the sacred, i.e., what is set aside and consecrated to God, were all good, this would be an easy matter. However, a brief review of church history, or any contact with a local parish, will prove such a simple generalization to be untrue. Many important things come in mixtures, and religion is certainly no exception. God could have created a neatly separated secular-profane, good-evil world, but he clearly chose not to do so. This unclear mixture requires both the atheist and theist to be on their toes against deception and oversimplification, and it also tells us something about God. In the first place, we learn to be careful

41

in attributing unity and simplicity to God himself. Not that these classic qualities are not present and important in the divine nature, but in an era which takes its start from atheism they cannot be as dominant in God as they were once thought to be. Why? Because our age has discovered mixture and complexity where it is perfectly possible that the divisions could have been more clearly defined and neatly separated. Thus, we are clearly dealing with a complex God, or a simpler and neater world would have been selected. For instance, the sexes could be more mutually exclusive than they are. Today we let the mixture of good and evil, in both the secular and the profane, tell us something about a God who must himself have a slight preference for complexity as against simplicity.

Those persons who are devoted to or involved in the religious life have an easier time within protected monastic walls, and as a result they often tend to see the world in an unbalanced perspective. If you are involved in a religious life for the right reasons, you see the good in it and also the good that can be accomplished in the world through it. The very idea of religious involvement or religious vocation means the concentration of energies in a certain direction. When one is surrounded by calm and beauty, it is easier to "see God," particularly if one experiences any healing power there, whether for himself or for others. The problem where God is concerned is that the world is so much wider than the small sphere of the religious, important as that may be. Atheism is forced on us precisely because we see the world in whole perspective and find destruction as well as healing, ugliness as well as beauty, and the agony of torn bodies as well as the calm of constant prayer.

Any adequate concept of God must conceive of him as God of the secular order too. That is why atheism is indispensable in forming a concept of God, since otherwise our view tends to be built simply on a sacred perspective, i.e., the world seen as the religious life presents it. Here is where theology desperately needs philosophy. If left to itself, theology will tend to build its concept of God on a sacred basis. This is easier for the theologian to do, but such religious construction must not be allowed to go unopposed. Even the devout man can be disturbed in his prayers

42

by the noise of the secular world, and then he needs a concept of God broad enough to account for those who are happily not at prayer and do not want to be. Philosophy, with its secular origins, offers the only basis for a view of God not artificially narrowed. To exclude philosophy is to run the risk of having a God not sufficiently powerful or complex to account for the power and goodness actually present in the profane sector.

Augustine, and many others with him, have focused on the world's beauties and harmonies and found their way to a God of similar perfection.* But those who are swayed by the force of atheism always point to the miseries and destruction in the world, and so the two arguments never meet. To stress the religious side of life too much is to miss the fact that what is secular is by no means bad or unenjoyable, and that is why so many can happily spend their whole life there. They do not feel the force of the arguments for God nearly so strongly as they do the pull toward atheism and pleasure.

Kierkegaard provides us with the interesting example of the lady who had been loved and left by Don Juan.** If her parish priest wishes to make her repent, he had better be able to preach the glad gospel of repentance with the same power of attraction as Don Juan preached the glad gospel of pleasure. We live in a world in which secular pleasure often has more strength and drawing power than religious repentance, and perhaps only atheism can teach us about a God who is sufficiently complex to account for this imbalance. Kierkegaard himself seems to fall into this trap. On one side, no religious writer is more aware of the power and goodness in the secular world and the mixture of it within the sacred. Yet when he comes to his devotional writings, their power and beauty are based on shutting out all the world except the religious and finding there an isolation and a quietude. This is the beauty of the religious life; its defect is that this exclusiveness is not sufficient when it comes to building a doctrine of God. Religiously speaking, God may be found in

*Saint Augustine, *On Free Choice of the Will*, A. S. Benjamin and L. H. Hackstaff, trans. (Indianapolis: The Bobbs-Merrill Co., 1964).

**Søren Kierkegaard, "Shadowgraphs" in *Either/Or*, Vol. 1, D. F. & L. M. Swenson, trans. (London: Oxford University Press, 1946), p. 163.

divine worship. Speaking technically, no new insight into God's nature can come from exclusive concentration on the sacred which is sufficient to counterbalance the force of atheism.

Secular life always seems clearer, easier, and more possible. Its goods are known and easily calculated, and along with this goes a clear, cold perspective on the mixture of evils to be avoided. The obviousness of secular life always give it an initial advantage over the religious. When you see that the goods of the religious way are less easily assessed, and that it is not pure but actually mixed with its own evils, this will certainly require a complex God if he is to account for such a situation and exert any attraction away from the secular. In this sense we have to admit that the sacred is "not good," in that it is not clearly discerned or easily practiced, and tends naturally toward impurity. This fact forces any argument for God to move "uphill" against a secular resistance.

If the sacred could always be clear and pure and strong, God might be easy to find and simple to argue for. That this is not the case is the source both of atheism's power and of our best insight into God's nature. Much that is secular reappears under religious garb. Much that is good is unassociated with the sacred and is strongly pagan in nature. Evil creeps into the sacred too, so that no sphere is pure. The true and the beautiful are not always good, which is a constant source of error and one that God must have deliberately included.

What keeps the arguments for atheism overbalanced is that the sacred can easily be invaded by the secular, but the opposite is not quite so easy. In fact, the sacred seems to have a tendency to decompose and degenerate if left to itself. This is not to deny either the power or the beauty of its insights, but simply to note its unstable nature. Of course, the sacred can be maintained, but it takes more constant attention and constant reform. On the other hand, the secular order seems always to be with us. Although it, too, can degenerate, secular cultures do have at least a natural tendency to grow and expand, perhaps drawn on by the obviousness of their pleasures. The secular easily invades the sacred; and when it does, why should anyone wish secular pleasures or natural evils to appear in clerical garb? On the other

44

hand, the secular does not admit the sacred so easily. In fact, it seems naturally to repel it, all of which weights the argument constantly in favor of atheism. *yes*

This leads us to reverse St. Thomas and St. Anselm to form a cosmological and an ontological argument against God. Thomas frames several versions of the argument leading from some aspect of the world's structure to God's existence, but each one makes the mistake of being oversimplified, and thus they are often without persuasive power. If you focus only on the order or the purpose or the design in the world, the cosmological arguments can lead to a God like that in kind. The only problem here is that the world is more complex and contains antithetical factors too, and these are left unaccounted for in the classical arguments. Disorder requires almost more attention than order and senseless destruction and waste are present along with purpose and design. If we actually reverse Thomas' arguments, they lead as easily away from God as to him. As St. Thomas admits from the beginning, it is always possible to be a naturalist and to admit no order greater than the natural. What we conclude from this is that, if a God is to be admitted, he must account for more than order, design, and purpose.

The same situation also applies to Anselm's ontological argument. If we begin, not from the cosmos but from the nature of God himself, everything depends on what kind of view of God we begin with. St. Anselm begins with "a being than which none greater can be conceived," but except for this one quality the rest of the concept of God is left unspecified. The movement of the argument leads us to see what this requires in the way of divine attributes (e.g., infinity, unity, no duplicate God), but of course its main force lies in considering whether that concept must of necessity include existence. Being has many modes and so, consciously or unconsciously, we must work out a clear view of the way in which God exists. If we do, the argument may have a certain logical sense, but it will still lack the specific detail necessary to give it real force.

If anyone who follows the ontological argument does not understand what is required of him in the way of specifying the mode of God's existence in detail, the argument may move away from God, and this is what it has tended to do in our day. We have not kept up our skill in thinking concretely about the divine attributes—a controversial issue and not an obvious matter as Descartes seemed to have thought. If the concept of existence we are using is inadequate, or if we fail to work out the details as we go through the consideration, the view of God posited will also be rejected as inadequate. No one will see any necessity to attribute existence to a concept of God which is not capable of accounting for the world as it is seen. If only all the possible concepts of God were one, the problem would be greatly simplified. Yet when we have two variables to solve for instead of one, we must try to shift among the concepts of God at the same time that we assess his existence.

We do not need to admit the existence of any being greater than the natural order, unless we agree to ask how this order was selected as against other possible ones. Our problem is that more than one being fits this role, and yet all concepts of God cannot exist simultaneously. Just as all possible orders of the world could not coexist and thus God had to make the choice of this one, so all possible concepts of God cannot coexist. The difference is that in this case it is man who must choose. Just as God had control over the possible elements that can go together to make a world and also had the power to choose with freedom among those capable of self-sustaining existence, so man is not helpless in the face of multiple concepts of God. He has a secular world to begin with, and any God must be capable of making the choices which were necessary to constitute this in the first place. We also have behind us a laboriously assembled tradition about God's nature that helps us by guiding us to the more likely concepts. Tradition only hinders us if it blinds us to the new choices possible.

What does this world of ours require for its explanation? Either one God or none. "None," if you do not see the world as simply one among all the possibles and ask how it got the power of existence over other equally possible orders. "One," if you do not accept the world at face value and inquire as to what kind of God is capable of constituting it as it now is in the face of all that was and is possible. All this only sets the problem for

46

us, but at least it has a focus, and this is more than some problems have. We know that only one concept is to be chosen, although we also know that many concepts of God will have varying degrees of possibility. Some may fit the basic requirements for creating the world even if they do not quite describe the actual creator. We can be satisfied with one who at least could create a world, although we are constantly driven beyond that to keep asking how to define the one concept of God which alone is actual.

Of course, in dealing among possible concepts we must come to understand the nature of theory, of terms and concepts, and of the language in which they are expressed. Thought and language may grasp the same concept in more than one way, so we have to allow for the degree of multiplicity which our intellectual medium itself creates. Still, this does not relieve the philosopher of his most difficult task, i.e., trying to grasp in communicable concepts the object to be expressed, and to do this in the most precise form possible. Here again we face a bias in both the secular and the sacred. The religious mind tends to use concepts which may be unacceptable to those who are not religiously affected, while the secular mind tends to favor concepts which often exclude any religious interpretation at all. The prize goes to the writer who can properly capture the mixture of both. That is, he must express a concept of God not wholly drawn from the realm of the sacred. It should be one capable of giving greater strength to the profane while yet identifying completely with neither one. We need a concept of God capable of being simultaneously sacred and secular, behind both and identical with neither. A wholly sacred concept may be personally more comfortable to the religiously inclined, but it is less accurate theologically.

From studying atheism's naturalness we have learned that we must be prepared for added complexity if we introduce a God. Scientific theory seems capable of sustaining added complexity for the sake of achieving a greater theoretical flexibility, but atheism is strong precisely because adding God to the theory actually increases its difficulty. Ockham's razor tends to cut God out when every hypothesis is eliminated if it is not necessary, although the crucial term here is "necessary." Is the added complexity of God necessary for greater accuracy, so that God must not be cut out, and we must learn to cope with a greater complexity of theory rather than with less? We once thought the easiest and the simplest were to be preferred in theory, but even if we have grown in sophistication beyond that point, we still have to recognize that the weight is on the side of atheism from the beginning.

When we assert that God deliberately chose the order we see, while rejecting all other possible combinations, it is actually more difficult to accept the world as it is. That someone should have intended all that we find, that evil should be so closely mixed with good—all this requires more justification if a God exists and not less. Of course, in the end it may still be a fascinating theory, and it might explain the mixture of good and evil in a more comprehensive way. In earlier times we seemed to have the idea that to accept God solved problems and relieved some intellectual difficulties. That was when we saw the world as without alternative. In other words, as we have ourselves increased our understanding of just how flexible the structure of the world is and how many alternatives there are to it, the naturalness of atheism has also increased, and this fact is the major source of our contemporary problem.

When we accepted a fixed order, it was not unnatural to argue for a fixed concept of God. Now that any one order for the world no longer seems necessary, just as our view of the variety of possible worlds has increased, so also has our understanding that more than one concept of God is possible. This complexity has multiplied at a fantastic rate. It makes atheism now a far simpler solution, and a concept of God more difficult to arrive at and less obvious to justify. The only necessity which our age seems to know is the necessity of an alternative to everything, and it is more difficult to justify God's choice when we know that it could have been otherwise. What cannot be otherwise, that we do not hold a man responsible for, as Aristotle explained. Now we are forced to hold God responsible for a great many unpleasant features, once we know that they need not have been as they are. We can correct many of them, and so also could God if he had

48

but chosen to. When we did not have this basic contingency to contend with, it was easier to settle on some one necessary concept of God. Our situation in relation to God is fundamentally changed in a modern, contingent world.

There is too much innocent suffering in the world which any simple, good God would not include, so that if we are to have a God he must have ulterior motives. To recognize this is easier in some senses than to think we have a fixed concept of God to begin with. Now, if some features are irreconcilable with a particular concept of God, at least we know that the concept can be adjusted. A God bound by necessity had a certain firm quality about him, but such a concept will no longer do for a world of contingency which seems constantly to be turning into a neighboring possible world. A God capable of handling contingency and of accepting the vast horrors resulting from the decisions it requires—such a God is more fascinating, provided that you can ever arrive at the point of belief.

In dealing with God we face unequal pressures. No one's mind can ever be forced to affirm God's existence (although the unbeliever's body can be killed), but you may actually feel compelled to deny him. The same conditions which tend to break a man drive him to atheism. The Jobs of the world are exceptions, and suffering beyond all bounds, whether observed in others or felt in oneself, strains belief to the breaking point too. A more profound faith may result from a crisis, but the point to note is that the pressures placed upon a man are not equal, and in themselves they favor atheism. To suffer and to know that it need not have been, or to observe the world's misery but be unable to do much about it, while knowing that God could have and chose not to—that drives a man toward atheism in ways in which no argument for God can ever exert an equal pressure. The sacred when experienced in itself may be pleasant and may make belief in God easier. Its mixture with the profane, and the force and violence in the secular world which always threaten to break in—these factors keep the sacred from ever being a safe road to God.

If only the concept of God had concreteness, a mind might move toward it and find in it a pressure equal to that of atheism.

49

Suffering and inhumanity are concrete and brutally solid, whereas God does not even hold still in concept. If our thought of God at least had the kind of stability which concepts can have, i.e., to be one clear idea, that would be little enough as opposed to the terrors that crush man and argue for atheism. Yet our concepts of God must be fixed over and over again, and this makes their lack of concreteness all the more pronounced. If our idea of God were firmly fixed, the mind might conceivably be taken by storm and enough pressure exerted to offset the drive of atheism. However, God as an object shifts in concept, and this situation must first be stabilized.

If the present and past are taken as a whole or evaluated at any one point, no matter how momentarily favorable, this does not seem to favor a simple concept of God, and thus religion is driven toward the *future* for its explanation. This does not in itself solve all things. There is so much to be accounted for in accumulated terror that any future explanation is going to have to be rather drastic. If an argument for God always involves the future, it can never be too forceful, and it will have to depend upon a number of contingencies not yet assured. Any given individual may, of course, believe this future promise, just as Hume argued. That is not the point. The point is that when a future as yet unknown and unfulfilled is appealed to, immediately the odds are against such belief. David Hume thought this sufficient to reject the possibility. Since we live in a slightly more precarious world than Hume's, we accept the fact that a long shot can win and that what is unlikely may in fact be true.

If the future turns out to be exactly like the past, God is certainly an unnecessary luxury in such a scheme, since his existence or nonexistence changes nothing. Either for a given individual or when taken as a whole, if any future improvement comes about solely as a result of human effort, a God might exist only to enable us to thank him for allowing us these possibilities. Still, this is not a very important or crucial part of any scheme unless we want it to be. Only if God himself acts to produce such a change can that changed future itself argue for God's existence; but as long as this action is still in the future, it can be believed in but cannot be appealed to as evidence. The divine action might not occur in fact to produce the change, since there is no necessity in it. This means that a contingent future promise cannot force belief until it has actually taken place.

How can an argument, then, be based on an as yet unknown future? This is especially difficult if that future state is alleged to be different from a known past and is not the result of what man has within his power, but comes through some radical reconstitution by God. Again, one may believe this to be true and may argue for it in the sense of explaining it, but certainly it cannot form a persuasive piece of evidence for one who does not care to believe it will happen. All the evidence of the accumulated centuries of an unchanged past are on the side of the one who doubts the argument based on the promise of a new future. There is no reason why the future might not at some point become radically different, as Hume said, but this cannot be argued on the basis of either the known past or the present moment.

In looking at the past or in predicting the future, improvement and accomplishment appear to rise and fall according to favorable or unfavorable winds, and also because of human effort or the lack of it. This situation in itself argues against the existence of some concepts of God, as regards both past action and future intervention. Those who are religious, of course, do believe that some divine intervention has occurred in the past, and often they find it in the present in their own lives. We cannot deny that this might be true, but the problem is that it simply provides no evidence to those who do not see it or feel it themselves. It is an argument which depends on individual impact. This obviously is forceful only for the individual who undergoes it, since by admission it is not a universal experience.

The sacred, then, is based upon a future hope. Believable as this might be, it would be more credible if things sacred were not always so involved with the immediately secular. Just to the extent that they are, it becomes harder to believe the future possibility due to the present intrusion of the secular into the sacred. This impurity tends to make religion appear very present- and not so future-oriented. To the extent that those who are religious testify to their future hope by means of their good acts in the secular domain, the promised future becomes

51

more credible. However, good and evil are presently so intertwined, and atheism so strong, and the future so impossible to touch with one's hands, that any simple theism still has the odds against its being true.

Pt. of this Ch. is that good & evil is such a complex fact of life, that God must be big enough to embrace the complexity — or less real than the complexity. To be proven active amid it, & we cannot escape the logic of the present by a 'pie in sky' future. Insupport too for God.

Evil ∴ constitutes a major obstacle to faith.

CHAPTER V

The Death of God

Any announcement of the "death of God" is, of course, a sensationalist statement in search of a shock effect, but still it may be instructive to examine the meaning contained in such a pronouncement. A classical concept of God is one in which he cannot by nature pass into and out of being, since he is said to be self-existent. The "death of God," then, in this case can only mean that one has ceased to believe in that concept—not that what cannot die has passed away. Certainly it has always been possible for someone no longer to believe in the existence of an eternal and self-existent God. Furthermore, a person who once believed may cease to believe, and this is a very meaningful way in which God can be said to die, i.e., that someone who once believed now no longer can. As far as the individual is concerned, this certainly is a "death of God," since a God who once was alive for him now no longer is. Even if God does not pass into and out of existence, belief in his existence certainly can.

Of course, the situation is not quite so simple. We do not have one agreed and complete concept of God which always remains constant and about which we assert either existence or nonexistence. Any conversation or exchange with God is made difficult by the fact that there are so many concepts of him. Nor is it even as simple as having a finite of infinite set of concepts, each fully elaborated and clearly developed. Our views of God vary; they blend into one another. As befits the object, each has certain indefinite aspects and remains somewhat incomplete. This being

53

the case, the only proper reply to any announcement of the death of God is: "Which God?" It would seem impossible to prove that a being corresponding to each of all the possible concepts of God could in fact not exist, since you would have to examine an infinite number in order to do this. It is a perfectly natural and healthy phenomenon for some one concept of God to "die," and it also tells us a great deal about our relationship to God.

Since the only way to deal with God seems to be by examining concepts about him, and since the number of these tend toward infinity, the most meaningful questions concerning the death of God are two: (1) In what sense can a concept die, and (2) in what sense may God himself be said to change form so radically that this alteration amounts to the "death" of an earlier form? Since a concept is never the object itself, but instead merely stands for it, one real sense in which a concept can die is when it loses its power to direct the mind to the corresponding object. For it is possible for a concept to be very closely associated with its object; when the word or words are heard, the mind is so immediately directed to the object that there is no awareness of passing from one to the other.

This, unfortunately, is never true of God, or for that matter of any difficult concept or object. In the case of God, there are problems involved in asserting that the object is ever fully grasped. Even where it is simply a matter of the concept that stands for God, we have already pointed out that such a concept is seldom fully understood, especially in view of all the alternative concepts which continually suggest themselves. We are dealing with a situation, then, in which the object is seldom if ever fully grasped, and one in which the concepts of it seem to be in constant formulation and reformulation.

Any given philosopher or theologian, or any individual who becomes one, may stabilize and develop a concept of God, and this may achieve such vitality that through it other minds are directed toward God. When this happens the concept has power. It may rightly be said to be "alive," since the exercise of power is the central meaning of life. In the case of God, this does not mean that all who examine the concept will understand it in precisely the same way or will always be led to the same degree

54

of apprehension of God. Such uniformity of grasp is not possible in this case, and yet the concept is "alive" because it is possible for it to have power to direct a mind at certain times and places. When wide numbers of people come to recognize this power as present in the writing of any man, his concept of God can rightly be said to be "alive." That concept may even become what we call classical, i.e., capable of sustaining itself in the literature and continuing to possess this power even when at certain times it is only latent as it waits for future sensitive readers.

Why do concepts which were once alive die or at least lie dormant for a time where God is concerned, and what does this tell us about our theological situation? That concepts may lose their power and "die" indicates first of all the multiplicity of concepts with which we are dealing, such that one tends to shade into another. Faced with such a multiplicity of concepts, in order for any one of them to be "alive" it must cut through this multiplicity and give the mind an ability to focus on God. Since there is nothing necessary either about any concept or its ability to do this, circumstances may shift in such a way that any given concept can no longer accomplish its aim, or at least its power may be weakened and its ability to direct lessened.

Most important, concepts about God have a tendency to lose their power if left alone. They seem to need to be surrounded by a more complete philosophical perspective, and also they require a mind familiar with the kind of concepts involved in any discussion of God. Concepts, of course, may die in either of two ways: by becoming so unfamiliar that a mind can no longer be oriented by them, or by becoming so common that the words tend to be accepted on face value and no longer incite a mind to search. Sustained familiarity usually breeds impotence where concepts are concerned.

Concepts of the divine have a particular tendency to lose their reality. As suggested, perhaps this is due to the special difficulty of the object and the multiplicity of the possible concepts. Thus, concepts of God require a greater than ordinary effort to sustain their vitality. The framer of the concept must try to keep it from shifting into some related concept, and he must give it enough precision to hold the mind directed toward God. Our minds

55

apparently turn away from such a difficult object and back to more familiar sights unless they are held there by a concept capable of sustaining its direction. The fact that a concept is able to accomplish its task once does not at all guarantee that it can do it again—that is, unless care is taken to revitalize it from time to time.

Concepts are rejuvenated by being reinterpreted and also by being placed in new settings and given a different context. Thus, to reinterpret a concept is not so much to alter it as to save it from increasing impotence. If placed in new surroundings, a classical concept may regain its power to direct the mind, but it will not necessarily retain that power if simply left alone. In fact, if not occasionally redone, it will tend to die. If a particular concept of God should die through neglect in any age, there are still quite a few others which may continue to exist. We have no shortage of concepts of God, and it is hardly possible that all will simultaneously be pronounced "dead." However, it requires an age of metaphysical and theological vitality to keep very many concepts in force at any one time.

Understanding why concepts of the divine tend in themselves to die, and what kind of revitalizing effort is required to counteract this—all this leads us to ask if there is a concept of God that actually permits him to die, once having been alive? We know that most traditional concepts are such that God's death is not possible, although it is true that a God corresponding to any given concept may never have existed, or it may be that the concept itself experiences death in losing its power. Still, a concept of God could be such that his death would be possible—but then we must ask what kind of God this is, and whether such a concept is religiously and theologically adequate? Such a God would, in the first place, not be self-existent, nor would he have sufficient power to prevent his own extinction. Under these circumstances, it seems hardly likely that he could be responsible for the creation of the universe, and this makes him not a single first principle but at best one among several. Such a semipowerful God is not very impressive or useful, given the extremity of our situation, and you cannot be much more saddened by his death than by that of any man. We need a God more powerful than that, or we may as well have none at all.

Yet the issue still remains: Could God change form so radically that this change would in itself amount to a death? The first thing to note is that, as long as he continued to exist in any form at all, this would not be "death" in its most extreme form, i.e., annihilation. It would be more like a metamorphosis. This, of course, may be what some of the death-of-God theologians actually intend to assert. Anyone can deny, which certainly is his privilege, the traditional Christian concept of the resurrection of Christ, although it is a rather central Christian doctrine. You can assert that God changed form, died in the body of Christ, and was transformed into an immanent God who now operates within the process of the world. This also involves a denial of the doctrine of the Trinity, since traditionally God was not wholly existent in Christ alone. He only became incarnate while still remaining the Father and the Holy Spirit, independent of Christ.

Still, all this is possible, if you want to form a concept of God such that he is capable of, first, becoming fully incarnate in Christ, and then changing further upon Christ's death into a power immanent in the world. However, the crucial factor is to determine whether a God like this can himself control such a transformation or whether he is the victim of it. If he changes uncontrollably and is dictated to by external forces, such a God (i.e., one who is essentially helpless to prevent his own transformation) cannot really be a very helpful deity, since he cannot even save himself. His death or transformation is not of great concern to us, although observing the process might be of some mild curiosity. The forces which dictate these changes actually become the real objects of attention, and we should search among them until we find that which controls both itself and the transformation of God.

God might die, in the sense that he changed form radically, but then we must ask if this is a God who can really be an object of religious worship? If not, we are back to sorting out and constructing from among all the possible concepts of a self-sufficient, self-existent deity. This, it is true, raises the problem of pluralism. Are there really many Gods, equal in number to or slightly fewer than the many concepts? Since many of the concepts actually overlap and are quite similar to one another, it is highly unlikely that so many similar Gods exist, but there might be at least a plurality of distinct Gods corresponding to the infinity of related concepts. Now, just as with a God capable of changing so radically that the change amounts to a death, we have to ask if a multiplicity of Gods is actually acceptable in theory? Without rehearsing the long metaphysical tradition which has tended to allow only one first principle, at least we ought to note that the plurality or singularity of God is an issue that requires early decision in any theological consideration.

On the face of it, a God who is one among a plurality of Gods would seem to have more chance of dying than a singular God, i.e., one subject to no external challenge. Still, if there is but one God, nothing prevents the concepts of him from being multiple. If true, this would account for why we tend to think of Gods as multiple, since we are influenced by the actual multiplicity of the concepts of the one God and the impossibility of settling on any concept once and for all to the exclusion of all others. In the face of such a situation, we should first set out all the reasons for preferring one concept of God over the other possible ones, although we can never be sure that we have arrived at the one concept which perfectly fits the one God. In fact, given the nature of words and the tendency of concepts to die, this can never happen. However, at any given time a concept which is constructed powerfully enough may actually be able to lead the mind to God, or at least to his vicinity.

Of course, when Nietzsche proclaimed the death of God he understood this question in its classical theological setting, and in our day it would be both simpler and clearer if we put the question back in its traditional form when we consider it. On a trinitarian account, Christ is also fully God, so it has always been a matter of debate whether God participated completely in all aspects of human existence. However, this hypothesis encounters its most extreme questions in the crucifixion of Christ. If Christ died upon the cross, can it be said that God died too? This has been an issue since Christianity's beginning, but the majority of theologians have stopped short of declaring this ultimate participation in humanity dramatized in the form of God's death with Christ.

It is hard enough to account for God's participation in the many other human aspects of Christ's life, so that theologians have tended not to involve God in humanity's death. If we see the "death of God" as merely reopening that issue, the controversy is entirely different and not quite so sensational. We can follow a more radical course, which has some historical justification, and assert that in the incarnation God assumed human form even to sharing in death. Affirming this, of course, does not solve an issue, but it does set the problem clearly.

Such a statement has much that can be said for it as a very orthodox interpretation of the doctrine of incarnation. The classical formula that "what is not assumed cannot be saved" should apply most of all to death, since it is Christianity's assertion that death is first and foremost what God conquered and transformed in Christ's sacrifice of his life. To have God able to suffer death on the cross is a rather radical interpretation of Christian doctrine, but it has merit to it, and it is not really either heretical or atheistic. Actually it is a more profound rendering of a very ancient belief about God's nature and action. To put the death of God in this setting is to see it, not as a new assertion, but as a reinterpretation of a very traditional concept. Of course, everything depends upon the concept of God you have and the interpretation given to resurrection.

To assert of some Gods that they died with Jesus on the cross is of course not possible, since their nature (e.g., eternal, immutable, etc.) is such as to make this impossible or to render the assertion of it very difficult to comprehend. Thus, in order to go along with any assertion of God's death in Jesus' crucifixion, we need a newly developed view of the nature of God, such that an extreme sharing in human qualities is not ruled out from the start. Then, the next question concerns the resurrection. A God who may die but who has the power to overcome death and to transform death in doing so—this is a very interesting and powerful God. Our trouble, however, is that precisely the doctrine of the resurrection is what our age has been least able to believe. God might have become immanent in nature at the moment of

59

Jesus' death, but it requires a rather special view of God's nature to picture a God who would act in this way. In which direction are we to move now?

What this question brings to light is that the issue of the death of God, when it is put in this way, drives to the very heart of Christian doctrine. In the assertion of the death of God by crucifixion, all the central Christian doctrines come to a head and require solution. You must determine Jesus' relationship to God, and you must also know the nature of God in order to determine his possible participation in death. In the concept of the resurrection, you see the capabilities or the limitations of that concept of God, and you define precisely your relationship to the central beliefs of Christianity. The question of the death of God is at the heart of orthodoxy, and in solving that classical question a tradition is given its contemporary reinterpretation. In order to do this, however, a clear concept of God must first be developed, and it must be capable of sustaining an argument raised on this level.

Why has the "death of God" recently been the cause of so much confusion, when—as indicated above—it might have served as a focus for clarifying the concept of God? If we understand the assertion as indicating the inadequacy of one concept and as advocating and prompting the formulation of a more adequate view—or if we see it as raising the central problems of the Christian doctrine of the Trinity and the resurrection—then to consider the death of God might be the most constructive enterprise of our day. Of course, the first explanation of the source of confusion here is that theology is tied to religious belief, and to open up any question about God will always seem to some to threaten faith itself. Without its connection to the emotional life, religion would have no power to move men either to good or to evil. Thus, discussion in this area will always be colored by irrational reaction. This is a difficult circumstance, but it is also an indication that we are touching something important for human beings.

In our day, what makes the situation even more subject to confusion is that we have not kept up our ability to discuss and to structure a theological issue by using a clearly developed

60

contemporary doctrine of God. When the issue of "death" is introduced, if we had a new concept of God under construction, the various problems it raises could be set in context carefully and then discussed. As it is, we seem to have available only the once powerful but ancient concepts of God, plus some few new views of untested value, so that the issue generates more emotion than incisive discussion. The "death of God" is not meaningful in isolation but only when placed in a metaphysical context—but we have to be able to produce that context.

That we often cannot provide the right context in our day is as much the fault of the philosophers as of the theologians. For some strange reason, Kant does not seem to see the difficulties involved in constructing a concept of God; instead, he concentrates on what he takes to be the epistemological problems of how a traditional concept of God can actually be known. If we shift the primary question from metaphysics to one of theory of knowledge, we are prevented from undertaking the metaphysical exploration necessary to uncover what might be a more adequate concept. Since Kant's time, most men have tended to take the concept of God for granted and then simply to argue about its difficulties. This is an appalling state to be in, when you consider the vast number of existing concepts of God and the difficulties involved in arriving at a satisfactory one. In such a situation, it is hard to keep God alive.

Of course, with Nietzsche there is another question involved in addition to his traditional understanding of the problem of whether God suffered death with Jesus on Calvary. Nietzsche takes his start from that issue, but what he really wants is to remove God from the scene completely. The "death of God" is also the beginning of a militant humanism. Some men will kill in order not to occupy second place. It is always humiliating to be inferior to any being and equally exhilarating to be second to none. Nietzsche values such human expansiveness, and he is willing to destroy anything that stands in its way, including God. This is not the place to ask whether Nietzsche's and humanism's trust in man is misplaced. The point is that, for Nietzsche, God must be opposed because he limits man. How man is placed in relation to God depends entirely on what concept of God you are working with, but rather than adjust his concept Nietzsche preferred to destroy it.

In this respect the "death of God" also challenges our whole view of man; God must die when man wants to be God, to occupy his place, and to exercise his powers. Nowadays most men have lost their taste for playing God, but Nietzsche had not yet come to a state of resignation. In appraising human freedom, it is essential to see whether our view of man is such that it is compatible with God. God may be either useless or inhibiting or a competitor of man, so that in any announcement of God's "death" we must look for its implicit view of man. God and man are the two variable concepts in this formula; but if we have been inhibited metaphysically from developing new concepts, we tend to have a metaphysics which is dictated for us, and it may be one uncongenial to God's existence. Then we become helpless in the face of the question of the "death of God."

Metaphysics really means to uncover and to consider the basic principles assumed in an argument, and the "death of God" is full of philosophical presuppositions. What this controversy points to more than anything else is the metaphysical vacuum of our day, so that when an issue requiring metaphysical reconstruction is introduced, we do not know what to do with it. If an issue arises which challenges basic assumptions, to debate as if the concepts involved were fixed and admitted no alternatives is not to produce fruitful change but to increase confusion. The "death of God" is too dramatic a way of phrasing the problem to be accepted for what it appears to assert. Like most dramatic formulae, it contains within itself a complex of important issues.

The death of God can lead to the birth of a new concept, or it may lead to the absence of any concept at all. Surely this decision should not depend upon a concept of God which few men would wish to accept, as if it were a question of this God or none. While it might seem that this controversy leads only to the strongest atheism and antireligious hostility, if placed in a different context it can provide a profound understanding of the religious concept of death before rebirth. "He who seeks to save his life shall lose it. He who loses his life. . . ."—this might be turned back to apply to God too, although traditionally it has not been done. Since, as we have agreed, concepts of God have a natural tendency to lose their power and vitality, he who clings to one concept and refuses to let it go may, in seeking to save it, actually kill it. Whereas, if we are willing to let a once hard-earned concept of God "die," as concepts can, perhaps the experience of absence is the only possible situation in which a new concept can be born.

Ours is a dangerous day, in which Gods as well as men live with the constant threat of death. Yet the divine participation in death is precisely at the heart of the Christian message, except that it also continues to assert the overcoming of death. This cannot be done unless we have a concept of God sufficient to back up such an assertion. Thus, if God is lost today, it is because our extant concepts of him cannot support the traditional Christian assertion of the conquering of death. In this day, one in which death threatens both God and man, a new concept of God may be born when God's death is announced, but we have not yet witnessed God overcoming death again in our time.

ie. God must be big enough to truly embrace death, yet overcome it in resurrection life. We've not yet managed that one - either we cannot allow God to in fact die; or he is dead. It's all over.

63

CHAPTER VI

The Existential God

If it seems strange to link atheism and faith together, the only reply is that this is precisely one of the major problems of our age. In spite of some negative predictions, religious interest and even fervor have not died out, but rather have if anything increased. Yet coupled with this is perhaps the strongest impulse toward atheism in recent generations, and it reaches even to the theologians. This is why the problem of atheism is not a simple one. If only many or most men merely espoused atheism quietly, it would not constitute a problem, although it might be upsetting to some theistic groups. Instead, however, interest in and sympathy for things religious remain quite strong, and many find some form of faith a possibility. When this is coupled with potent factors that lead toward formal atheism, such a peculiar combination of atheism and faith deserves to be labeled a problem.

In order to try to understand this strange mixture, Soren Kierkegaard ("S. K.") is a good test case. S. K. represents a rebellion against established orthodoxy, and yet a religious profundity and sensitivity have developed around him which fueled a religious revival almost singlehanded. The most influential modern exponent of existentialism, Sartre, is clearly himself an atheist, and yet he holds Kierkegaard responsible for much of his inspiration. How is it possible for so deeply religious a person as S. K. to inspire so strongly atheistic a follower? What is there

64

about Kierkegaard's writings that makes it possible to follow him and yet end up in atheism? It is hard to read him without appreciating the fresh vitality he gives to so many religious concepts. Sartre shows a tendency to follow him in his psychological explorations; he even phrases problems in the revitalized religious terms learned from Kierkegaard (e.g., sin and dread). In spite of this, Sartre has a distinct tendency to systematic atheism. Why? To answer this we must understand Kierkegaard's God and his relationship to Hegelian metaphysics.

If you read S. K.'s devotional literature, it is hard to imagine more beautiful or more orthodox and serene writings. There is not a shadow of doubt here. His *Edifying Discourses** are meant to be just that, to edify their readers in a conventually pious sense and not to disturb them. His God is a classical God of immobility and majesty, and the human spirit who approaches him is comforted, quieted, and supported. Not much is said that describes God directly, but it is easy to see from the mood and tone of the religious writings what kind of God S. K. is addressing, and he is a very orthodox and traditional deity.

In spite of all his interest in God, it is strange but true that Kierkegaard's strongest and most famous attacks are on metaphysics and systematic thought. It is clear that he identifies metaphysics with the brand of Hegelianism in which he had been trained, and "system" has only one meaning for him, i.e., the particular views of Hegel. In order to be free to express his thought, Kierkegaard had to rebel at this point if he wanted, as he did, to put the stress on "the individual in isolation." Kierkegaard did not intend to give up either philosophy or theology, but only to approach each in a new way. This seemed to him to require an objection to metaphysics and systematic thought, since in his mind these could mean only one view: Hegel's.

"Reason," of course, also meant the necessary and universal reasoning of Hegel, so that, if Kierkegaard was to stress the isolation and contingency of each individual, he could not do so without opposing reason itself. "Metaphysics," "system," and "reason" all seemed to S. K. to have only one meaning, as he had

what existentialism is

*Søren Kierkegaard, *Edifying Discourses*, D. F. and L. N. Swanson, trans. (Minneapolis: Augsburg Publishing House, 1943), 2 vols.

first understood them from Hegel, so that the only way to change them would be to oppose them all. To do this puts the responsibility back on the individual, and that is precisely where S. K. wanted it. He could not build a new view without first tearing down the old one, but the difficulty with this position is that his opposition seemed to require him to assert the impossibility of systematic thought at all. If it was hard to keep from being absorbed into Hegel's system, the only safe way appeared to be to deny the possibility of all systems.

Our question now is this: Is S. K.'s God responsible for the atheism that springs from Kierkegaard's religious setting (e.g., in Sartre)? The problem is that there is little direct discussion of God's nature by S. K., and this fits with his antimetaphysical polemic; i.e., he opposes formal theology and rejects the systematic basis from which new theological views might be generated. Still, any discussion of religious issues must have God in it somewhere, and to the extent that one can discern how Kierkegaard thinks about God, his God is very traditional in concept. S. K.'s God may love and suffer, but Kierkegaard never works out a new theory of the divine nature on these terms. Not that there is anything wrong about this in itself, but it must be considered in the light of the other elements in S. K.'s thought and the effect produced by their combination.

To know God in Kierkegaard's devotional writings is to meet one who offers rest. He is a God beyond anxiety, one who brings tranquillity to the soul. He is a generous, a loving God, one in whom the worshiper can lose himself. Even outside the devotional realm, S. K.'s God is infinite, eternal, immovable, etc. For all his challenging of conventional thought, S. K. does not even suggest that the orthodox view of God which he inherited should be revolutionized in any way. He has many religious problems, but one of them does not seem to be how to conceive of God. On the contrary, the tension in his thought arises precisely because of the contrast between the view of God he holds and the rather new psychology he develops. Kierkegaard alters his view of man, but not of God, so that his religious question is how to reconcile a traditional God with a radical view of man and his condition.

66

The problem of theodicy never troubles S. K. either, and this fact is also significant. When he speaks religiously, all justice is on the side of God, and there is no hint of a question about God's dealings with man or any urgency to demand an explanation for the rather severe conditions present in the world. Not that Kierkegaard is out of line here; he is at one with his inherited tradition, but the rest of his thought is not—there's the source of the problem.

Even if evil is left unexplained, Kierkegaard's antisystematic and antimetaphysical campaign is the most serious factor that leads to the separation of elements in his thought and tends to convert his religious fervor into Sartre's atheism. S. K.'s thought is radical at its most influential points, and this really does not fit in very easily with a traditional view of God. S. K. might have worked to construct a new view of God, one more suitable to a radical age, but his antimetaphysical tendency prevented this. He cannot allow himself or others to do such systematic work —driven as he is by a fear of being forced to Hegel's conclusions.

This dilemma is particularly clear when we consider his antirationalism and his extreme individualism. "Reason" meant necessity and determinism for S. K., and he opposed it in the name of contingency and freedom. Although he placed the responsibility for decision solely on each individual, Kierkegaard could have built a view of God consistent with this. In order to do so, however, he needs a metaphysical base and a systematic intent, but he excluded these in his reaction against Hegel.

It is consistent with existentialism that S. K. should leave each reader free to form his own conclusions about God, but is the situation more extreme than that? Are the elements of Kierkegaard's view needlessly incompatible, so that the struggle of the individual to hold them together is excessively difficult, and thus these elements in his thought actually tend to break down and lead to atheism? For instance, he uses as the central illustration of the "paradox" involved in faith the Christian doctrine of the incarnation. Given his existential view of the nature of man's existence, it certainly is paradoxical for a very orthodox, eternal, and unchanging God to enter into a human existence of this kind. Kierkegaard never challenges the unrevised view of God's

67

nature that makes the incarnation so rationally incomprehensible. A man of intense religious disposition will hold on to his faith in spite of paradox, but eventually the tendency will be, either to revise the view of God in light of the new understanding of man, or to accept the view of man and reject an inharmonious God. Those who are without a strong religious disposition naturally will move in this latter direction; they are propelled toward atheism by an outmoded religious view.

The most novel aspect of Kierkegaard's thought is his use of psychological terms and his analysis of "the individual." His concept of God is not new, and placing his God in the midst of such novel views actually produces the paradoxes of faith which S. K. feels so strongly. Someone not religiously inclined will recognize the novel elements in his thought, and then find his God so dull and conventional as not to be worth the effort which belief demands. Kierkegaard's God in *Fear and Trembling* is capable of irrational action it is true, and this is never explained in terms of God's nature. Such metaphysical description simply does not come naturally to Kierkegaard. When he does describe God, as in *Purity of Heart*,* he is traditionally serene as an object of devotion.

Sartre naturally rejects a dull God who does not seem to fit this novel psychological situation. This is most evident where the problem of evil is concerned. In a pious setting, Kierkegaard does not raise the classical question of theodicy, and a naturally religious person may simply accept evil's presence without complaint. One who is not by nature religious demands the justification of God's ways to man, but S. K.'s God has nothing to say on this subject. Released from the power of the author who holds them together, the stronger elements in S. K.'s thought rise to prominence and the weaker ones (his God) recede. Thus atheism is a natural tendency, and the problem of evil speeds the dissolution of his religious power.

Kierkegaard rejects historical study as being unable in itself to lead man to God. Man never becomes contemporary with a past event, although there was a time when he thought he might

*Douglas V. Steere, trans. (New York: Harper Torchbooks, 1956).

achieve this. Faith must concern the present and the future, Kierkegaard correctly sees, and it will be found in this direction or not at all. How ironic, then, that his view of God is one of an inherited and historically oriented diety. S. K. failed to see why it is that we must form a concept of God by looking forward too. This is because he rejected metaphysics; he thought of it as necessarily historical in its orientation. In rejecting speculative metaphysics, he lost the only means by which he could possibly develop a new concept of God with a future orientation.

In *Fear and Trembling*, Kierkegaard gave us a new account of man's classic struggle with God, which at least in Abraham's case ends in faith.* Faith is portrayed as believing the preposterous and setting oneself against the world and its laws. Because he intends to sacrifice Isaac, Abraham is a murderer in the eyes of society and a man of faith only in God's eyes. Yet S. K.'s problem is that, perceptive as this account of faith may be, he does little to explain God in this connection, i.e., what kind of God it would be who would act in this way. S. K., of course, wants to make the mark of faith our willingness not to demand an explanation, but that would be easier to follow if God himself were not a problem and did not first require an explanation. It is impossible for Kierkegaard to tell by any external sign who is a man of faith, but the problem is that all this is compatible with many different views of God, including some which Kierkegaard would probably reject. What Kierkegaard overlooked is that there are more Gods than one, and faith has meaning only in relationship to a given concept. You must first decide which God you are going to believe in before you can even surrender your demand for explanation.

Abraham's action, Kierkegaard is sure, cannot be understood by any observer. What God is like, however, is what determines whether a religious man's faith is understandable or not. It would seem that Abraham cannot be understood, primarily because Kierkegaard has never given us a description of God's nature in terms of which an action can be understood as either consistent or inconsistent with that view of God. The fact is that faith is

*Søren Kierkegaard, *Fear and Trembling*, Walter Lowrie, trans. (Garden City, N.Y.: Doubleday–Anchor Books, 1954).

only radical in *Fear and Trembling*, due to S.K.'s failure to tell us a little about what God is like. If he were introduced, God could relieve some of the pressure which is put on faith; Kierkegaard's faith remains extreme because he keeps his God's nature hidden. S. K. begins by saying that faith means to struggle against God, and yet faith becomes blind because we are never told precisely who we are up against. Kierkegaard seems to know this, but he makes it difficult for others by never telling us what his God is like and why this makes such human struggle a natural reaction.

A subjective and individual struggle with God, which is faith, does not deny that there is an objective issue about God. In fact it presupposes it. It is just that, as S. K. prefers to define it, Christianity is restricted to mean subjective appropriation by the individual. Kierkegaard is sure about his God's objective content, and thus the issue is only one of acceptance. Today our problem is reversed, and we have no content—or else we do not know which one to use—for the idea of God, and so the subjective question of faith seldom even gets raised. The Kierkegaardian urgency over the subjective question of personal appropriation misses us completely. Before Christianity can have even a subjective existence for the individual, it is necessary to pose the problem of God objectively again in such a way that it will raise a subjective problem for the reader.

God, S. K. is sure, realizes the conformity of thought with Being, but for an existing spirit truth is always in the process of becoming, and no such identity is realized. The trouble with this metaphysical view is that it is dogmatic. That is, this might be the case, but although Kierkegaard has analyzed it pretty carefully for man through his psychological investigations, he nowhere justifies or expands this view of God. Thought might conform to Being for God, but then again it might not. If you reject systematic construction, the power and ability to explore metaphysical alternatives is also lost, and then an inherited statement has the appearance of being necessary without alternative. What this does is to make a succeeding generation eliminate God as an unelaborated and anachronistic metaphysical assumption, whereas a God who was revised on the basis of S. K.'s insights into human psychology might have a greater chance of survival.

When the situation is constructed so that there is no way that the several irreconcilble parts of a view can be held together, then the dividing line is sharp: mysticism for those who insist on giving up nothing and atheism for those who feel that to hold a certain metaphysical view is not in itself necessary. Kierkegaard's "religiousness"—i.e., paradoxical religiousness—drives one toward atheism when you realize that there is nothing at all necessary about accepting the kind of God involved there. Then you either employ metaphysics, which S. K. cannot bring himself to do, and work out a new theory of God, or else you drift naturally toward atheism, propelled there by a theology unaware of its alternatives.

To be fair to Kierkegaard we must understand that he does not care whether or not great numbers of men actually do drop God out of their thought. Christianity is both rare and difficult for S. K., and belief in God is made to involve paradox and absurdity precisely to insure that only a very few will have enough energy to embrace it. Yet if we now turn to consider Sartre, what we have to try to understand is why it is more natural for Sartre to eliminate God than to go to all the trouble involved in keeping him. Sartre is not flippant about this. To give up God causes him at least as much pain as it does for S. K. to keep him. Sartre thinks human existence would be easier if there were a God, and still he does not believe in one. This is not because he rejects all absurdity, since Sartre actually is willing to accept much of Kierkegaard's equally difficult analysis of human existence. As far as developing a rational system is concerned, Sartre could just as well accept God, and yet he does not. To understand why he does not is perhaps to learn something both about the sources of atheism in our own time and about a possible "existential God."

On the nonsystematic side, it is important to note that the external circumstances for Sartre's existentialism are almost the opposite of Kierkegaard's surroundings. Kierkegaard learns an Hegelian orthodoxy of speculative metaphysics. Hegel is gone in Sartre's time, and the closest Sartre can come to metaphysics is phenomenology. Kierkegaard lives in a stable, upper-middle-class society which is conservative in its ways, while Sartre witnesses France's collapse and occupation and the disappearance of most traditional and conventional standards. S. K. thinks that everyone grows up an automatic Christian, whereas Sartre finds himself living in a very secular society. Kierkegaard takes an orthodox theological view of God for granted, whereas Sartre sees no reason to accept such a view and is personally not inclined to build up another God to replace the traditional one who has disappeared. Both stress psychology and literature, but in external circumstances their times could hardly be more different.

This contrast does, I think, help explain why Sartre feels no necessity to develop a new concept of God and why Kierkegaard was inclined to keep his God in spite of the absurdity and the paradox generated by putting an ancient God in a novel human setting. Existentialism becomes a humanism for Sartre, whereas it was a religious view for S. K. Sartre's precise claim for humanistic existentialism is the virtue of a "greater consistency" in eliminating God. This is an interesting comparison, for Kierkegaard knew all too well that the presence of God made things difficult rationally. The once overly rational Kierkegaard turns and challenges reason, whereas the Cartesian rationalist Sartre finds in existentialism a means to preserve reason in a violently irrational age. S. K.'s age was too orderly and rational, and he said time and again that it was reason alone that needed to be opposed. His psychological analysis of human existence does this, although Kierkegaard's psychology is out of harmony with his metaphysically rationalistic age. Sartre's outer world is in chaos, so that an existentialist view of man preserves reason individually when it is not present externally and universally.

Given this situation, God is essentially a hindrance to Sartre. Sartre finds no God in his inherited external order, since S. K. generated no new view of God to go with his existential understanding of man, and an inherited God actually makes Sartre's aim to rationalize human existence all the more difficult. Kierkegaard wanted to introduce absurdities into a too-complacent human existence, and an ancient God was helpful for this pur-

72

This all shows that despite Kierkegaard great ideas, he had no new view of God ∴ not a prophet - & no new voice of Scrip.

pose. Seeing absurdities reign all about him, Sartre wants to do the opposite, i.e., to render human existence rational. God hinders this aim, or at least the God he inherited from S. K. Sartre might have developed a more compatible idea of God, but given his aim, he had no reason to want to do this.

Strange that, for Sartre, God's existence is a threat to man precisely because he too sees God in a conventional sense as a being possessed of complete foreknowledge. For Sartre, to exist before God would be to determine man completely, and so God must be rejected in order to leave man free to define himself. Just because Sartre is so much a rationalist, he must reject God on the grounds of consistency, whereas Kierkegaard accepted God in spite of the absurdity of his rationalism in the midst of an irrational world.

Kierkegaard had no interest in forming a new concept of God, since it would have robbed him of his major point if such a God had been consistent with his understanding of existence. Later existentialists might find God helpful to introduce order into chaos as they actually want to do, but S. K.'s God robs man of freedom if his existence is accepted. Given the choice between an old idea of God or none, it is much better to force man to "go it on his own."

Existentialism begins with Dostoevsky's point that if God does not exist then everything is permitted. Kierkegaard's God does not determine human action, but if he were rationally consistent he should. In demanding consistency Sartre must reject God in order to get freedom. We are "condemned to be free" because we are left alone. Kierkegaard's man is alone too, but only because the God who is there cannot be reconciled with human existence and thus is of no help in human decision. Sartre is unwilling to achieve man's freedom through Kierkegaard's absurdity—at least the absurdity of an incongruous God.

In *Being and Nothingness* Sartre gives us detailed analysis of the meaning of Being.* He could have turned this into a new analysis of the nature of God, but Sartre considers the new psychological concepts in detail, and sees no reason to extend

*Jean-Paul Sartre, *Being and Nothingness*, Hazel Barnes, trans. (New York: Philosophical Library, 1956).

73

them to God. Sartre has a new metaphysical base and at least a mild systematic intent, but rejecting Kierkegaard's God actually has certain advantages for a rationalist, and his existentialism alone does not require him to become a theologian. Certain religious concepts can be kept without God, and the existentialist analysis of "negativity" supports these while not requiring a God. Besides, Sartre still labors under the traditional assumption that to introduce a God is to eliminate contingency and freedom and add irreconcilable conflicts, which is what God does for Kierkegaard.

If a novel view of God might have been produced, why couldn't Sartre see this possibility? What else besides metaphysical timidity and a failure to look beyond tradition in theology can explain this? If one theological problem seems to obsess Sartre, it is the problem of theodicy. He is painfully aware of man's failure and of the evil and destruction in the world. An inability to reconcile this human picture with a view of God leads Sartre to reject both God and any attempt to construct a more congenial view of God on a new metaphysical base (e.g., his own analysis of nothingness). In his age of stability, Kierkegaard has a God, but he is one apparently not concerned about the presence of evil. Sartre is upset about evil and he has no God. He never attempts to construct either a new God or a new theodicy.

Kierkegaard has an amazing lack of awareness of the problem of evil and of God's relationship to it and to human depravity. Existentialism in its twentieth-century setting, on the other hand, is filled with such awareness. Sartre's investigation of "the origin of negation" can be the metaphysical counterpart of the awareness of destruction and evil which his plays stress, but he never explores this possibility. Kierkegaard's God is acceptable, so to speak, until the question of evil arises. Then, in the face of chaos, S. K.'s God dissolves and we are left with atheism. Sartre's inquiry leads him, as he says, to "the heart of Being," and it is really only here that the problem of evil can be dealt with.

Kierkegaard developed new psychological categories, and it is through understanding man that Sartre investigates Being. Man faces the permanent possibility of negativity, and nothingness as a structure of the real gives rise to this. In posing any question, since it may always be rejected, a certain negative element is introduced into the world. In this sense it is man who is responsible for nothingness, but what is man like, Sartre asks, that through him nothingness comes into the world? Freedom is man's power over Being, i.e., to modify it and to introduce a nothingness which isolates him; only in anguish is man conscious of his freedom. Here Sartre draws on S. K.'s analysis of anguish, and if Kierkegaard had done something like this he might have developed a new theory of the divine nature.

Anguish comes through an awareness of possibility, i.e., that no conduct is necessary. Nothing compels you to adopt what is merely possible. The self you would be you are only in the mode of not-being, and this realization induces anguish. Since man is always separated from his essence by nothingness, he is not compelled to become it, since it is only possible. This means that anguish is a manifestation of freedom. It is always possible not to do or to become what you intend, and this realization produces anguish. Yet this is also the very condition for the possibility of doing what you will. Here freedom shapes being, but "passing through" this state is not a necessary process, and you always face the possibility of losing yourself in nothingness.

Consciousness means to be conscious of the possibilities of nonbeing and of the nothingness internally present in any being which constantly threatens it. Consciousness means simultaneously to be what it is not and not to be what it is. You are what-you-are-not through the mode of negation (as Plato pointed out in the *Sophist*), and you may always lose what you are because it is not necessary and can pass over into nonbeing at any time. Freedom is the experience of this and it produces anguish. When Sartre takes the step toward systematic inquiry which Kierkegaard rebelled against, it immediately becomes clear just how different this analysis of Being is from any traditional God. As long as S. K. refrained from systematic effort, he could retain his conservative God, although it required paradox and absurdity to do so. The minute Sartre elaborates this kind of analysis of Nonbeing, it becomes clear that a traditional God is by his nature completely out of place. God must be such that he could create man and the structure of Being in which he exists or else God serves no useful purpose.

Traditional philosophy usually gave an analysis of man closer to the categories of necessity and being. As long as man is considered under a mode of Being, he might be reconciled with God in some way, even if God were fully necessary, etc., whereas man is not. However, when the basis for the understanding of man itself becomes freedom and nonbeing and anguish, then there is no way a traditional God can be responsible for such a radical creation. If God cannot explain human existence as it is analyzed, certainly there is no need for his existence metaphysically.

If a classical concept of God cannot be the result of Sartre's philosophical explorations, granting that his method and his aim do not lead him to one, what kind of concept of God might come out of Sartre's context? What follows at this point, and what I want to give now, is an argument for God built upon existentialism's strong natural tendency to atheism. This will yield us "the existential God." This is not to say that Sartre himself "ought to have had" such a God as I now want to develop for him, or even that such a view is the only one which might be worked out on Sartre's basis. I simply want to try to see what kind of God existential insights can lead to. Granted that Sartre's analysis quickly causes him to deny a traditional God, if one reverses these tendencies to atheism, what kind of view of God can be built on these same existential foundations?

In order to answer this question we might begin as follows: Negation is the starting point and freedom is the primary concept for understanding an existential God. In the pursuit of Being, Nonbeing is discovered to be the foundation of Being. If we convert this to the question of the search for God, it means that, in seeking God, Nonbeing is what is first discovered. Then how can such nonbeing—and the experience of it—provide the foundation for the discovery of God's being? Consciousness, in questioning its relation to God, discovers not only that its being is in question, but that so is God's. Thus, if God's being were certain in every sense or were ever grasped without any doubt, we would never discover this fundamental feature of God's being. Since in man's being his being is in question, and since God's being is too, this approach leads us to discover Nonbeing as also fundamental to God's being. This fact we might have overlooked if God's existence were not first subjected to doubt by the power of atheism today.

If either our own or God's being were certain, we might fail to discover this fundamental negation, and then we would be unable to explain the negative forces in the world. Whenever we ask the question of God's existence, an immediate negative element is introduced. We face—both at that moment and always—the permanent possibility of a negative reply to every question asked. God's existence always remains in question, since the asking of the question of God's existence, no matter how it has been decided at any previous time, can always be answered negatively whenever it is posed again. For this reason, the first element encountered in considering God is always negativity. In this way the arguments for atheism lead to a new conception of God which could not be discovered if his existence were not constantly in question.

Asking the question of God, however, leads the questioner to the heart of Being because the problem of negativity has now been raised. Yet every question presupposes both a being who questions and one who is questioned. This does not in itself establish a God but merely the fact that, in questioning Being, a "ground of Being" emerges. If the being who is questioned remains silent, the always-possible reply is "nothing" or "nobody" or "never." Since a negative reply is a permanent possibility, the first relationship set up between God and man is one of nonbeing, i.e., the nonbeing of knowing in man and man's apprehension of the possibility of the nonbeing of God. If we ask what the first result is of questioning God, the answer is: an encounter with nothingness. Thus, if the being of God is ever to be understood, it will arise out of, and be based on, a prior understanding of nothingness. To understand both God, the questioning of God, and the questioner of God, you must first come to grips with nothingness. It is always possible that you may stop here and never discover either your own being or God's, or only the first and not the second, but there is no way around this danger.

77

The only route to God's being is first to encounter nothingness.
The permanent possibility of a negative reply whenever one
asks the question of God's existence leads to the permanent
possibility that one may stop in negation and never move from
it. This original nonbeing sets the limits for any reply which is
possible to the question of God, for what his being will be must
of necessity arise on the basis of what it is not. Nonbeing is
discovered to be real, and any description of the reality of God
therefore begins with nonbeing. *The problem of the nonbeing of
God must first be settled before his being can even be discussed,
let alone discovered.* What are the senses in which God can be
said not to exist, what elements of nonbeing are present within
God, and what could his being be, so that in encountering it the
first experience is always of negativity and nonbeing and nothingness? *Atheism finds its foundations in the negativity which is
permanently present whenever God is considered, and any new
understanding of God's being must have its origin in these same
negative roots.*

Sartre discovers that it is not negation which is at the origin
of nothingness, but, on the contrary, that it is nothingness as a
structure of the real which is the origin and foundation of negation. Thus, that God's existence is always in question and that
any questioner faces the permanent possibility of a negative
reply reveals to us the reality of nothingness as fundamental in
God's nature, or else we cannot explain the negativity which the
question of God gives rise to. The necessary condition for our
saying No when we consider God's existence is that nonbeing
should be a perpetual presence in us, in Being in general, and in
God. We search for that in Being (i.e., Nonbeing) which accounts for our experience of negativity.

If human reality is the emergence of some particular being in
the midst of Nonbeing, God's reality must be discovered just as
being emerges from nothingness. Anguish is the human mood
which comes from this awareness. It arises psychologically because Being is continually threatened with a return to Nonbeing,
and because God can only be understood by passing through
nothingness. He who knows no anguish cannot know God. Since
the being of God remains always in question, anguish cannot be

78

overcome. It can only be understood as fundamental to our experience of God.

A serious question is only possible if negation has a basis in reality. To ask the question of God itself presupposes negativity as ever present. To solve the perpetual presence of negativity here means to understand the existence of nothingness within the being of God which itself is the foundation of the negativity that constantly surrounds his existence. Here atheism is a better teacher than theism, since it begins by bringing the negative elements to our immediate attention. To begin to consider God on a positive basis may restrict us from the start, because it enables us to account for only a part of Being. This jeopardizes the existence of God because it makes him unable to account for the force which negativity has due to its origin in nothingness.

How can God be related to nothingness so that through him nothingness comes to us? Sartre thought that man introduced negativity; now it proves to be God who is responsible. Such a being must have the form of his own being in question, so that through this nothingness is introduced. But what can it mean to say that for God his own being is in question? His existence may be always in doubt to us as questioners, but that is a trivial sense, except that we have agreed to locate in the being who is under question the source of the possibility of a negative reply. The amazing thing is that, where God is concerned, his being and the negativity surrounding it are greater than that surrounding the being of man or of any object in the world. How can God in himself have the form of his being in question, so that this might explain the doubt in man where God's existence is concerned? Sometimes being is in question because it can pass into and out of existence. If this is not the case for God, in what real sense can his existence still be said to be constantly in question?

God's existence is always in question in the sense that the issue over what he will create and under what conditions he will do so is forever an open question. Since no necessity governs his creation, any single condition in the world might be different, and man reflects this contingency in the constant uncertainty over his affairs. Only nothingness compels God to create, that is, the threat that if he does not create one order then nothing will exist. Yet nothingness does not compel any one particular kind of order to be created. Thus, any existing order is always haunted by the awareness that it need not have been at all, or at the very least that it need not be in the way that it is. For what he creates, man bears the responsibility, although he is always tempted to take refuge by blaming some necessity. Negativity is his only coercion for what God creates, i.e., the flight from nothingness to some form of being. Yet, since absolutely nothing needs to be, everything that exists bears the mark upon it of its contingency and of its relationship to nothingness in the decisive action of will which alone enables creation to take place.

Thus, God's existence is in question in that he does not create out of necessity, and he bears the responsibility for what does come into existence when any aspect of it might have remained in nothingness. The reasons behind his own action are a question to God, and therefore his existence in this sense is constantly in question, since nothing in his nature leads him precisely or unavoidably to exactly this form of creation rather than that. However, as with man, to understand in greater detail the elements of God's nature is to recognize the internal factors which lead in one direction rather than another. We learn what excludes certain possibilities, and this narrows the range of choice. If necessity connected God to this particular form of creation, the mind would be led from nature directly to God. In the past some have argued that this is true, but it does not seem to be true today. Atheism is the testimony that God's relationship to creation might be different and that a simple contemplation of nature does not lead of necessity to one God who had to create it in that way. Negativity leads us to the presence of nothingness. Inquiring into the nonbeing in God, as the explanation of the nothingness encountered, leads us next to the contingency of God's activity. His freedom continually places his being in question.

To be able to question, you must disengage yourself from being, so that the danger involved in all questioning is that you will remain permanently detached perhaps even from your own being. Yet Being is discovered only in questioning, so that the risk of the loss of being in disengagement is itself the necessary condition for the discovery of future being. Since God's creation

80

is not necessary, he must question himself, disengage himself from his own being, face negativity in his own being, and answer the question "Which form of being?" by overcoming the tendency to nothingness which his questioning introduces. He opened the way for man to question his own or another's being, because the very being of the world originated in God's questioning of himself and thus still retains its connection to nothingness.

God is the being through whom nothingness first came into the world, since from nothingness the world first came to be. This is a new meaning for the doctrine of God's creation *ex nihilo*. We now know enough to reverse the pre-Socratics: From nothing something comes; that is the explanation of the world. This means that nothing forced God to create this particular order. Yet only the threat of the dominance of nothingness unless he *did* create forced God to question which possibles to bring to existence—to detach himself from his being in questioning—to encounter nothingness in such detachment—and then through it, and in spite of it, to create something.

Something comes to be from the fact that nothing had to be. God's flight from nothingness does not force him to only one creation, just as our flight does not either. Anguish is experienced when God first faces nothingness and then is forced by it to act and to create, and yet he is not determined to one particular act or creation. Freedom enters in at the origin of all things, and our consciousness of it is reflected by anguish in both God and man as each faces the structure of Being.

We do not always experience this in encountering the world, since we can take our world for granted as simply being what it is. When God's existence is in question, interestingly enough, nothingness and anguish and negativity cannot be avoided. To ask the question of God is to cast a question over the whole of existence; it is to cast the cloak of nothingness over the world in a way that questioning the world does not always do. Contrary to Sartre's thought, man introduces negativity into the world of necessity only when he questions God's existence; only through the natural tendency to atheism is Being revealed. Of course, man may introduce nothingness into his own being or into the

81

world by questioning anything at any time, but it is interesting that only the problem of God raises the question of nothingness inescapably.

This is why many who read existentialism reply that they do not find the world so difficult or so full of nothingness and hence negativity. The world and man may produce this experience or even nausea, but neither does so of necessity. If the question of God is raised properly, however, negativity is necessarily introduced, since it is possible to take the world and everything within it for granted, but this can never be the case with God. Thus, the anguish which Sartre introduces is properly a religious anguish over the lack of fixity in the world's form; this arises from its dependency on God's determination to act and to decide in the face of the possibility of nothing at all.

When Sartre's questions are addressed to a traditional God, no reply comes, and then the philosopher may speak in the name of Being as Sartre does. However, from the anguish that springs from the experience of nothingness, a concept of God may also be formed. If so, it will be one which accounts for atheism's naturalness and one that locates the origin of nothingness in God himself. Existentially it is possible to escape from anguish, and the world can be accepted at face value—except where God is concerned. Then negativity, nothingness, and anguish cannot be avoided, and a God will be found through them or not at all.

If God is the being through whom nothingness first came into the world, what must God's being be in order that through him nothingness may come into being? First, God must question himself, hold the whole infinite range of possibles up simultaneously for consideration, but in doing so he puts himself outside of all actual being. Here we discover the meaning of the traditional assertion that God is "beyond Being." In holding all possible beings up for consideration, he places himself outside of Being, thus calling Being's form into question and placing his own nature next to nothingness.

If this is true, Being's structure is never necessary as we discover it. It is first weakened by being subject to question, originally by God and then by man ever since creation. Through questioning, man discovers that he can modify Being's structure,

82

just as God originally gave it some one definite form only through questioning himself. God modified the absolutely infinite range of possibilities to give our universe the form in which we find it. Man modifies Being's form in questioning it; he bends it back toward the range of possibles from which it originally came.

God has the freedom to give the order to Being which he wills, and this spreads the element of nothingness into the world. In relation to Being, man can only feel meaninglessness if the world's meaning and form actually are not necessary but contingent. This being the case, meaning comes for many only as it first did for God, i.e., by a free act and never from necessity. This freedom isolates God from man and man from God. God in questioning and acting places himself at a distance from the actuality of Being, since it need not have the structure it has. Man isolates himself from the structure of Being which is given to him, and also from God, either when he calls Being into question or when he refuses to act upon the alternatives presented. This questioning often leads man to atheism, because he experiences deeply the negativity which is so much a part of the world. If carried through and properly explained, it may lead to a new concept of God, but, of course, the one thing this consequence cannot be is a necessary one.

What is God's freedom, so that through it nothingness comes into the world (as well as something), and so that it sets for man his greatest difficulties and opens up anguish and despair? Man's fall is ultimately to be traced to God's freedom and not to man's, since it is from God's freedom that the possibility for negativity originally comes. God is free to give reality to some forms of Being and to exclude others, since all possibles cannot come together in existence. In questioning Being, man discovers God's free choice at the origin of our present form, and then he understands why every question is capable of a negative answer.

God's freedom dealt with nothingness, but it also unavoidably included nothingness in the foundation of Being. *Freedom is ontologically anterior to Being and makes some particular form of it possible.* In this sense existence precedes essence for God too. Freedom and being are identical in God, in that it is not possible for God to exist without exercising freedom, and man could not be unless God were first free. To exist as an object, then, first requires of man a decision, just as God's free act precedes any coming to be of Being.

Kierkegaard's God does not know anguish, but the God which Sartre could have discovered can feel it. Freedom is impossible without anguish, for anguish is excluded only where necessity is present. Thus, all necessity—although real—is derived, and strangely enough it derives from freedom. Anguish appears when all necessity is discovered to rest upon and to be derived from some previous free decision. Anguish is present in God because he does not even need to discover this fact by encountering negativity in the world; God's anguish is based upon his primordial free decision to have this order rather than that, these potentials rather than any of the infinite variety actually possible. Man is never without some criteria in his decisions, and neither is God, but none is sufficient to determine either this exact decision or only one result. The responsibility for the order created and the mode of being adopted is first on God's shoulders and then on man's. This produces an experience of anguish over freedom for both.

All conduct is only possible and never necessary, although the degree of necessity and the range of possibility may vary upon occasion. God's anguish, then, is the greatest that can be imagined, since his range of possibility is absolutely infinite and his decision necessarily finite. Nothing compels God to act. This is true in the double sense that not to create at all leaves all worlds in nothingness and no thing exists to limit God in his choice. Man's experience of nothing is less total, and this is just as well. A face-to-face encounter with the nothingness with which God deals would—if he were left unprotected—destroy man in its fury. The future exists in man in the mode of not-being, and it causes anguish because it is impossible to be identical with or certain about the future one wills to be. God, in questioning, placed himself in anguish by creating what he did, and then he stands necessarily at a distance from it and from us.

The meaning of freedom is the permanent possibility of abandoning the project you have set out upon. Nothing compels you to be what you will to be, and this nothingness, which is my freedom, also separates me from the essence we all drive our existence toward. In God this anguish is controlled, and thus it never destroys him, since his power is great enough to sustain *omnipotence* any decision made. Often man can neither control his decision nor sustain it, in which case anguish may destroy both the man and his freedom. God could abandon his specific decision, but he will not. Man often wants to abandon a decision and cannot, or often wants to sustain it but lacks the power. Man's freedom in that sense is wider than God's, but God's freedom is greater in the sense that his power is sufficient to sustain his decision just as if it were an irrevocable necessity. The values of the world are founded in freedom, i.e., man's freedom to reject them by setting himself at a distance from any value by questioning it, and God's freedom to constitute one set of values in the face of both nothingness and the infinite range of value norms which might be.

Now, after this metaphysical and theological exercise, we must conclude by asking: Would Sartre recognize an existential God such as the one described above? The answer is that he should at least recognize him, although he is certainly free not to acknowledge his existence. This is, we assert, a view of God —or the beginning of one—consistent with the existential analysis of human psychology. The traditional view, such as the one Kierkegaard retains, was not, and Sartre was right in rejecting it. However, if atheism is always the necessary first step toward building a new concept of God, theism would not be possible without Sartre's exploration of negation, nonbeing, and nothingness. Not that this is the only route to God, but if existentialist thought has had a natural tendency toward atheism, out of this condition the situation is ripe for the birth of a new concept of God. That such concepts wax and wane is itself evidence of the nonbeing which is the foundation of God's being. Freedom in God also frees him from any absolute identification with any one concept of his nature, although to determine which concepts are more appropriate than others is now man's free task.

To face non being was first God's Choice - before he created. Creation implies a choice on his part out of infinite # of alternation systems. If God first created nonbeing - & being out of it - then man does the same thru his questioning. And God does also embrace non-being in totality of reality.

85

CHAPTER VII

Atheism and the Theologians

Is it not cheating (an incensed reader might rightly ask) to take Sartre's doctrine, clearly atheistic in his own eyes, and construct upon it—even if only in a sketch—a theory of an existential God as I have just done? I took the arguments that led to God's downfall and attempted to ask: What new concept of God could meet the requirements which originally had the effect of excluding Kierkegaard's view of God? Such a procedure might not be fair if I insisted either that only one view of God is possible or that the view just constructed had some inescapable power to compel belief.

On the other hand if there are many possible views of God— we know not quite how many—it is actually folly to follow blindly a line of reasoning which seems to lead to the downfall of one view, and to think that this can result only in atheism. Of course, it does in a very minimal way, in that there is now at least one view of God which that person does not believe in. No line of argument, since it must be limited in its scope, can reject all Gods. Therefore, there always remain an indefinite number of additional concepts of God left to be examined after some line of argument has led to the rejection of one view. Our motto is: "Only one God rejected per argument, please."

Interestingly enough, Paul Tillich shares with Sartre his concern over theodicy, i.e., the justification of the ways of God toward man. In a special sense Tillich tries to construct a view of God which is forceful—rather than helpless—in the face of this concern over the destructive and wasteful power of evil. However, although it is a theme in several plays, this anxiety over theodicy is not so clear in Sartre's philosophical works. So far as ethical standards go, Sartre occasionally laments the absence of a God for purposes of understanding the source of value norms, but his systematic analysis goes on without much reference to the problem of evil or to the absence of God.

In his plays and novels the theological setting is much more pronounced, and this fact is significant in itself. In *The Devil and the Good Lord* the church is presented in its worst institutional light, while evil rages unchecked and the God referred to seems totally unable to cope with such destruction and the undeserved suffering of the innocent. The situation is so bad that man loses his feeling of guilt and transfers it to God. God should now ask man's forgiveness for the unfairness of existence, Sartre concludes.

Men suffer, and Sartre demands some assistance and relief from God. None is forthcoming, and so man must act instead and accept the responsibility for doing so. At the same time man rejects a God who is silent in the face of injustice. Sartre even suggests that we must approach the good Lord from the side of the Devil, but he never carries out such a suggestion systematically as I propose to do. Sartre simply sees God's absence and hears his silence and rejects him. He accepts one view of God unquestioningly and rejects it forcefully.

At this point Tillich enters and tries to deal with the situation as a theologian, yet he cannot be called a traditional theist, perhaps at best an a-theist. It is easy to see why Tillich is not a traditional theist, since that involves the God of Kierkegaard whom Sartre rejected. Tillich shares with Sartre and S. K. their view of the human situation, their love of freedom, and their rejection of anything that seems to degrade man. Joining Sartre in feeling the overpowering impact of evil, he also endorses Sartre's rejection of Kierkegaard's good, grey orthodox deity.

Yet when Tillich begins his positive construction, it is a difficult question to say just where he comes out concerning God. Tillich is a step closer to traditional metaphysics than Sartre, but (in working out his "system" he stops short of any of the ordinary

87

concepts of God. First of all, he is blocked by his refusal to make God an object. He learns from existentialism that to be an object is to be subject to mistreatment. Furthermore, the problem of theodicy leads Tillich to reject any ordinary concept of God as being inadequate to the widespread existence of evil so strongly felt in our own day. Yet the issue is: What kind of an answer is Tillich capable of providing from the nontheism he works out? Before this question can be answered, we must first examine the forces that drive Tillich's thought away from theism, and then appraise his success in working his way back.

Whenever theism is in serious doubt, one way to protect God is to place him above thought where words cannot touch him. Tillich consciously places his God beyond reach, so far in fact that he will not allow the name "God" to be used in any direct sense at all. Of course, he is not the first to do this. Such essential mysticism has a long history, from Judaism to Plotinus to Dionysius to Eckhart and onward. It is not hard to understand what may at first appear strange: that in an age of skepticism, mystical doctrine can have a resurgence. For, if such belief is hard to prove, it is equally hard to disprove. No arguments can touch a God who exists so beyond the reach of words, and a faith of this transcendent kind becomes possible again.

Such a tendency to reassert mystical doctrine in an age of skepticism has at least one essentially healthy aspect. Atheism is often brought about when a view of God becomes too prosaic or too mundane. Then it has no power to deal with the vast difficulties we see about us. When trivial views of God become useless, mysticism lifts our sights perhaps too high, but at least it reminds us of the difficulty of forming a concept of God—of his majesty and transcendence. Mysticism (the view that God is outside the structures of Being as known) of necessity moves us away from mundane views of God so that it may lead to a more vital theism. Unfortunately, it may also lead back to the same atheism it was designed to avoid. Why is this, and in what senses and in what ways has Tillich's thought tended first to lead away from contemporary atheism and then to lapse back into it? Mysticism as the opposite of atheism and yet eventually as leading back to it—this is a phenomenon among the theologians which we need to understand more clearly in our own day.

In all his thought Tillich tends to set up polar tensions, and he proposes a "method of correlation" in his *Systematic Theology*.* In doing this he gives valid expression to the double-sided quality we all experience in the world, but when it comes time to speak directly about God, a problem arises. If there is to be one God and not two, he must unite the polar tensions and include in one nature these qualities which are merely correlated in the everyday world. Since he avoids Hegel's dialectic method for reconciling opposites, Tillich's reply is no reply. That is, he does not give an explicit account of how these qualities reside and are linked together in God's nature.

Tillich's view, of course, is possible. The way in which God unites in himself these apparent opposites is a matter beyond logical description, because he believes that language is committed to and based upon polar structures and thus cannot escape them. The difficulty comes when the question of theodicy arises. On such a nonverbal, ultimately mystical view of God it is impossible to say much that is specific about God's intent or ultimate plan. There is little about such a highly transcendent view of God which enables you to "explain" or to speak very directly about the origin and future of the pervasive malignant forces which are so strongly felt.

"Theology" has traditionally meant the development of a view of the divine nature, and then from this to give an account of how God deals with the world. Given the a-theistic God which Tillich proposes, it is quite clear that theology can no longer do this, and he actually proposes to change the meaning of theology. Its object now is "what concerns us ultimately." In an age which cannot speak about God, existentialism has taught us to speak with new perception about man, and Tillich follows existentialism here. He rejects Kierkegaard's unreflective and orthodox God, but he moves beyond Sartre, not to atheism but to a mysticism which speaks little about God and more about man.

If theology's subject is said by Tillich to be man's ultimate concern, why is it that God cannot become an object? To under-

*Paul Tillich, *Systematic Theology*, Vol. I (Chicago: University of Chicago Press, 1951).

stand Tillich's revolt against allowing God ever to be an object is to grasp why he himself tends toward mysticism and why others who follow him can also tend to atheism. Existentialism is concerned with the depersonalization and dehumanization of man, and one of the main roots of this lies in objecting to ever making man an object like a rock or a stone. It is true, of course, that man could still be an object of a special kind and not be simply a "thing," but in violent reaction against the violent forces which threaten to destroy man's integrity, existentialism rejects every tendency to make man an object of any kind. This prevents men from degrading God, since he cannot be described foolishly if he cannot be described directly at all. Trivial views of God are ruled out, and that is desirable, but a detailed description which might have explanatory value where evil is concerned is also made impossible.

The prominence of a-theism among Protestant theologians today is a striking phenomenon, and anyone who wants to understand the problems of the day must seek out the causes for this situation. Any individual may be an atheist if he wants to, but an atheism prominent in theological circles is a matter requiring special explanation. Of course, it tends to be "a-theism" rather than a simple atheism. That is, it is not a radical denial of God's existence but simply a shying away from any traditional form of theism. It precludes any attempt to revise the tradition and then speak directly about God in an endeavor to create a more adequate concept. Of course, to explain all the forces that make theologians shy away from theism would demand a great deal and would involve all the forces that lead to atheism. Tillich stands as at least an example of one strong systematic reason why theologians tend toward a nontheism.

Many contemporary Protestant theologians follow Sartre and reject any simple view of a God who cannot deal with evil. Yet what is puzzling is that even theologians do not always move on to develop a more adequate theory of God. The philosophical views available in our time are either antimetaphysical or highly unconducive to theological extension.* Existentialism is theo-

*For a suggestion on how to deal with this situation, see my *The Future of Theology: A Philosophical Basis for Contemporary Protestant Thought* (Philadelphia: Westminster Press, 1969).

logical in its orientation, but unless it is radically changed,* it
tends to confine us to man and does not move us to God. Tillich
does move from existentialism to God, yet not to a theism but
to a mysticism which transcends it. Thus, existentialism as it is
extended by Tillich leads to a God but not to one who may be
spoken about directly or in any detail. Such a God may be
affirmed, but he may also be rejected, since he is incapable of
speaking out to answer the charges brought against him by man's
suffering.

This is the heart of Tillich's atheism, or a-theism, or nontheism: that he cannot allow God to be conditioned by the limitations of existence. This is a majestic view and is something which
simple theisms often lack. Unfortunately, it also works against
any theism, since it prevents the attribution of existence to God
in the sense in which it has been analyzed in man. Why is
"Being" too restrictive to be applied to God, you might ask? The
answer in Tillich's case appears to be that his understanding of
the nature of Being make it too powerless to allow him to extend
it to God. If he could begin with Being as applied to God and
then try to restrict it to apply to man, this difficult situation might
be reversed. However, Tillich gets his understanding of Being
first from the limitations of man; then, seemingly unable to rid
this concept of its defects, he would rather place God beyond
Being than restrict him by using this imperfect concept.

When a view of God is presented, men tend to question it and
ask it to produce answers that explain every evil in the world.
If the view suggested cannot do this, it tends to lead back to
atheism, and Tillich's God is rather silent (as befits him) on all
the crucial issues. This is not to say that Tillich does not attempt
answers to each problem, but we must ask: (1) Do these follow
directly from his view of God, i.e., are they suggested by it and
made intelligible in view of what God is? And (2), are the answers given sufficiently strong to meet the seriousness of the
problems raised? If the reply to (1) is No, the answer given to any
particular question may be accepted, but God will tend to get
rejected as being unnecessary to the view. If the answer to (2)

*For a suggestion on how this can be done, see my *The Existentialist
Prolegomena: To a Future Metaphysics* (Chicago: University of Chicago Press,
1969).

is No, this will be because the view of God did not supply them, and they had to be built up without the aid of God.

This tendency which Tillich exemplifies, to raise questions but to side-step direct answers, is perhaps the central phenomenon we need to understand in grasping the problem of atheism among theologians today. To develop a theory of God is to try to give specific answers, and this has always been the systematic function of a doctrine of God. Kierkegaard admitted that he merely wanted to raise questions without answering them, and yet, as Tillich rightly sees, questions often imply an answer. One man may simply raise questions, but, after a Socrates, then comes a Plato who develops from this a more complete view. When this happens, the points left vague by one man tend to get decided after him. Thus, for all Tillich's care not to be too specific, later on his thought will tend to be pinned down in one direction or another.

Jesus as the Christ is the bearer of the new Being—that is Tillich's central conclusion regarding Jesus, but again the description of Jesus must be symbolic for him. Exactly how the new being comes and what it means, this question tends to participate in the same mystical inexpressibleness that surrounds God's nature, and that is just what you would expect. The function of Christ is primarily to overcome man's estrangement from his existence, and it would seem that we are confined to existence and should not expect any radical transformation of its basic conditions, e.g., overcoming death. In developing his doctrine of Christ, Tillich actually speaks many more times about God. As we indicated, the solution to any major theological issue tends to require a more specific doctrine of God. Yet Tillich still refuses to take his more specific statements about God's activity in Christ as in any way literal, and this means that the actual accomplishments of Christ are surrounded by the same mystery that hides his God.

The tendency in Tillich is to limit all direct theological statements, and yet he does make some in spite of this great difficulty, just as Kierkegaard held on to his God in spite of the incongruity. It is quite natural, then, that those who follow him will find that the method employed leads them primarily toward man's situation and away from God. The existential stress on the primacy of human being as our entry into Being makes the movement toward God an unnatural although not an impossible one. The mystical God Tillich adopts is a possible solution, but the thrust of the movement of Tillich's thought is toward man and away from God. Unless a direct path can be found to God metaphysically, it seems that all roads may continue to lead away from him.

With Tillich we have one prime example in theology of how theism can turn to atheism. Unless a concept of God is clear and forceful, its abstractness causes it to fade and to lose its power. Ideas of God need constant renewal, both personally and intellectually, but the concept offered must be such that it makes this renewal possible. Some ideas of God can be arrived at once, but then it seems impossible to revive them. Is this the case with Tillich's God? And what can we learn from him about the natural tendency of theism to turn into atheism even within theology?

That Tillich's God may disappoint us is not at all unique to his deity, and understanding this tells us something about why theism naturally tends to atheism even among theologians. Few Gods offer to do anything very immediate or clearly visible about the wrongs of our world. This being so, their answers tend to be couched in terms of future promises which often are beyond any present individual's lifetime. This being the case, once a concept of God has been offered, we have a natural tendency to expect immediate results after coming to believe in it. Some less visible and internal results may in fact be experienced and change us as a result of belief, although often even these are not permanent and require constant renewal. When we observe that, to all appearances, the world is very much the same after believing in God as before, the excitement which arose on our first encounter with that concept of God soon tends to fade.

Of course, one may accept future promises and work for sustained internal renewal under the guidance of some concept of God, but the point is that our situation is such as to cause any concept of God to become disappointing. Either our clear grasp of the idea of God fades, or else circumstances once favorable to that God become unfavorable. Tillich is not unique in facing

93

this situation, but his "beyond-theism God" has even more difficulty in preventing this inevitable fate of all ideas of God, and
it tends more readily to atheism. The point is simple: a God who
cannot become an object is more withdrawn and less definite
even in concept. He is so little described or describable that, in
the face of the natural tendency of all concepts of God eventually to disappoint, it is hard to make Tillich's God concrete
enough to protect him against atheism.

If mystical doctrines have had great power in previous eras,
why not again today? In earlier times we did not mind having
a God who was not directly involved in determining the world's
contingencies. In fact, we once built a concept of God around
the idea of his being "unmoved." If contemplating Spinoza's
God only edifies us, so that we can accept necessity, or if Aristotle's God is merely a principle to explain motion, there was a time
when these were satisfactory functions for a God to perform.
Today we are more activistic, and this is not just as a matter of
fashion. We have discovered that a core of contingency—not
necessity—is at the center of the world's frame. We can ourselves change a great deal, and so we accept little as being
inevitable any more. In such a situation a concept of God, in
order to establish itself, must also be one which is itself able to
accomplish change. A transcendent God who merely bolsters us
by drawing us toward him tends to be rejected in a world which
is no longer viewed as necessary.

When we understand why a solution which is powerful in one
day (such as mysticism) tends ironically to lead in a different
direction in another era, we learn something about the basic
forces at work in our age. After learning this, some (e.g., Bult-
mann) have thought we must yield to these forces and construct
only a view which we find consistent with prevalent modern
ideas. That is to become the victim of a metaphysics, not its
master. Whenever we find a current concept (such as "modern
man") which seems basic to our thought, we do not assume it
and go on from there. Rather, the metaphysical instinct is to call
all first principles into question and to ask whether other assumptions are also possible. Only a metaphysics which considers itself
as necessary and thinks that the age dictates our assumptions can

94

be vicious at this point. Not that every metaphysical view is equally possible at any time, but we are not limited to only one in any age. Our job is to explore the range of those views, i.e., the alternatives that remain possible once we have uncovered some current reigning assumption. More than one theoretical system fits the facts, so that unfortunately facts alone do not give us our metaphysics.

Why, then, does mysticism tend to atheism in our era more than in others, and what does this teach us about the basic assumptions which are powerful in our day? If we cannot accept the frame of the world as fixed, when a God is introduced he must account for the particular order in which we find ourselves as against other possible worlds and the humanitarian improvements possible in them which even we can make today. A mystical God draws us away from the world and thus eases the pain of the problem of theodicy. Yet it does not explain it, and this gnawing question draws us back from mystical ecstacy toward atheism.

We can put up with evil and fight it and seek personal renewal even without God. Thus, if you are to keep alive a concept of God, you need one who deals with evil in decisive ways that are not within human power. *Theism tends to atheism when what God accomplishes can also be accomplished without him.* If he takes no decisive action in the face of evil, he is not necessary to the process, and someone less pious will soon come along to eliminate God as superfluous. If God is not decisive in the face of evil, then, thank you, "we'd rather do it ourselves."

The problem of atheism in Tillich centers in the question of his "Christianity." Mystical Gods have traditionally drawn their followers toward them, and such effect as they have had on men and human affairs is through the power of attraction they exert. Christinaity has asserted the opposite, i.e., the direct action of God without man's solicitation. According to this account, God came to man. Thus it is not a matter of what, in specific instances, Tillich still asserts that is traditionally Christian, but of examining his doctrine of God to see whether he is capable of radical action. If not, no matter how much you might wish to affirm Christian teachings, the view of God employed will work against them, and this leads to a rejection of that God. Whether Christian beliefs can be sustained will depend upon whether, as they lead toward atheism, these forces teach us the means to construct a more adequate theory of God, i.e., one capable of supporting Christian doctrine instead of working against it.

The view of God offered must be such that it is at least possible for Christian assertions to be true. In Christianity the assertion is strong that God has acted decisively in human affairs, but this is precisely the kind of thing hardest for Tillich to maintain. To enter human affairs means to become an object, and the kind of nontheistic God whom Tillich prefers avoids all such risk of degradation. Tillich's God cannot take risks; he cannot ask for punishment and maltreatment at the hands of men, but the Christian assertion has been that God did in fact risk this and made himself an object. The Christian God had hands laid upon him, and Tillich will not let his God become subject to the abuse even of concepts. Men do distort with the aid of ideas, but where Christianity is concerned, violence must be possible with our words about God, just as injury occurred when men seized him with their hands. God as an object must accept the risk of both verbal and physical abuse.

Tillich, of course, is not alone in having a philosophical setting —if it is not accepted—turned from an argument for God into one against him. Instead, Tillich is simply a case study in the influence of a philosophical context on an argument for God and of how a shift in that context may change the argument, so that what a theologian originally designed to lead to God now no longer does. We learn from this that an argument for God can only exist in a philosophical setting, and if that philosophical context is rejected, the argument has no force. For example, if we can accept Tillich's view that to become an object is always to be limited in undesirable ways, and that what is beyond all structure is to be preferred, then we can accept his "Ground of Being" as a God. Gods require a philosophy supporting them, and to provide this is a theologian's first concern.

St. Anselm and St. Thomas are no less good examples of this point. The outlines of Anselm's famous ontological argument are simple. Yet unless you can see the setting in which he means to

96

place it, e.g., the Platonic notion of dialectic and of increased understanding through consideration of a concept at first unspecific, so that the concept itself grows and is revised in the process—without this Anselm's argument may actually confirm atheism. St. Thomas begins by assuming that we must seek a first principle for all things. If his reader does not share this assumption, or if he does not feel as Thomas does that all contingent things must be reduced to that which is self-necessary—then Thomas' arguments can also induce atheism, since the required philosophical context is not present to give them force.

Unless a view of God is firm it tends to fade. As soon as you no longer see that the metaphysical situation needs to be as Tillich describes it, his concept of God will tend to fade too. If for instance you accept Plato's view that purposive motion is always the work of a soul, the universe as a whole tends to argue for a world soul. Such metaphysical assumptions need not be accepted, however, and if they are not, both the cogency of the argument and the firmness of the God tend to fade. *Such firmness as a concept of God has is given to it by its metaphysical assumptions, and its clarity and power are supported as long as that metaphysics is sustained.*

It might be instructive to ask: In what sense are Kierkegaard, Sartre, and Tillich all atheists? Kierkegaard is so only in the sense that his God becomes unacceptable just to the degree that his psychology becomes acceptable. Sartre is atheistic because he cannot find a God who is of any help in the face of evil and destruction. Kierkegaard's God can stay as long as the times are not severe. At first, human struggle was depicted as all internal, and if S. K.'s God did not fit the internal turmoil, at least he could be reconciled with external tranquillity. Tillich discovers a God who is beyond conception, but such a God can give no specific answers, and a completely contingent world demands a specific answer (even if not the only possible one) as to why things are as they are and not in some other way. We want to know what God intends to do about future contingency. "Atheism" means to have no God, and when these questions are asked, Tillich's God falls silent. To be unable to answer the questions asked is to create a situation conducive to atheism.

97

In discussing how concepts of God tend to "die," I have already pointed out one important factor which turns theism into atheism even in a theologian's hands. In Kierkegaard and Tillich's case we have tried to show what it is about their concepts of God that causes them to fade. This is not really a special criticism of these two men, since it is a general phenomenon and one which indicates again that we are not in an evenly balanced situation. That is, philosophy prejudices us to atheism, since any concept of God tends to fade under new conditions. To remain in theism is not possible without constant effort, since the natural drift leads you toward atheism if it is unopposed.

Yet in addition to the natural tendency of concepts about God to fade, there is one other quality about them which leads toward atheism. Theologians and others who write about God do not write what they see at the time but only how things seem in retrospect. When we consult our own experience, we are aware that this is true. It is only later that we realize and are able to say what has happened to us that is of decisive importance. The trivial we can grasp immediately. Looking back on seven years, say, we see what has transpired, and only then can we express what is crucial. But we often phrase this as the report of a contemporary experience—which it is, yet at the time we could not see and express it as such. The misleading element is that those who read such an account look around but cannot find in their own present experience what the writer describes as being in his. This ironic situation cannot really be otherwise, since the one who has experienced the decisive change correctly describes it as being in the present, although it can only be discerned in retrospect.

This, of course, is true not of every change but only of life's more profound ones, where the transformation is such that the significance cannot be taken in all at once. What happens is grasped in retrospect, and yet the concept of God appears to be contemporary. Actually, what its effect will be can only be seen long after the consideration. That is why to go through certain arguments may often seem to have no effect; later it may prove that their impact was not negligible. Thus, a concept of God may appear at the time to have little result because, by comparison with the way in which the impact of it is reported as being in the present, it cannot be felt so by the listening person. This discrepancy is disheartening, but no theologian can avoid it, and in the face of it there is a natural tendency to move from the unabsorbed concept toward atheism.

Those who follow later and see the words which have been written about God cannot see him as clearly in the present state as the words describe him, since those who wrote saw what they saw only in retrospect, in spite of their necessity to phrase their report as if it were something immediately seen. If we fail to take account of this necessity of understanding only in retrospect, a concept which once became real can now become unreal, because it is taken as a statement of present fact when it can only become evident in retrospect. Any action of God is seldom immediately seen, even though when it is seen in retrospect it is reported as if it had been presently observed. Here perhaps we are fortunate that the disciples did not take shorthand notes on Christ's life, for the record gives enough evidence that it did not become clear to them until much later what had really happened. Then, at a later time, they reported it as if it had been seen all at once in the present moment.

The odds, then, favor atheism, and even when theism is achieved it has a tendency to slip back toward its opposite. To hold a concept of God is not the easiest but actually the hardest thing in the world, particularly since the job is never done. If left alone, a God will turn into no God under the simple pressure of natural forces. Nor can any concept of God be equally adequate to all questions, so that, as the questions of prime importance shift in any day or for any individual, a once-powerful concept of God tends to become less so. A drift toward atheism is the most natural thing in the world, and to maintain theism is the most difficult task, even for a theologian.

CHAPTER VIII

The Metaphysics of Atheism

Atheism — or your attitudes toward God, etc. will be based on your metaphysical presuppositions.

Atheism is almost always thought to have a religious basis. Strange if we have discovered that its source is often metaphysical. Allowing for certain exceptions, the religious situation does not change greatly. God is neither any more nor any less easily seen today than he ever was. The occasional disgraceful behavior of his religious advocates may at times obscure this fact, or their charitable behavior may encourage belief. Of course, some assert that the rise of modern science has changed our religious situation drastically. Yet often it is not so much scientific technique and theory that have altered religion as it is the metaphysical assumptions which are associated with them. If naturalism or humanism or an evolutionary concept of theory are associated with any given scientific view, of course theology is prejudged negatively. However, no one of these is an obvious view in some necessary and inseparable association with scientific theory, so that often it is in its metaphysical assumptions and in its underlying first principles that science affects theistic or atheistic arguments most.

Exactly science presupposition

If, then, the climate of the twentieth century seems to favor atheism, this might be only because the metaphysics, i.e., the assumptions on which we operate, do not favor theism. If this is true, in order to understand atheism we must unearth the first principles of our day. To become conscious of our basic assumptions, since they are what are assumed and argued from and not to, requires a metaphysical sensitivity which is only acquired and

Thesis V

is not inborn. This is one way in which our age differs from others and where it favors atheism: that it has been—not exclusively but still very often—antimetaphysical. Being this way, we have tended to discourage metaphysics. When this sets in, we lose sensitivity about the possible variability of our assumptions. We become unable to reflect on them and instead take our premises for granted. *The Cultural Fact*

In addition to a loss of sensitivity to metaphysical premises (i.e., first principles which may be true but need not be so), an antimetaphysical temper favors atheism in the sense that its basic assumption is often that there is some one obvious theoretical framework which has now permanently replaced all others. This assumption is even more difficult to deal with than a weakened or atrophied metaphysical ability, because it is the one metaphysical assumption which takes its theoretical framework as exclusively true. As long as we admit the variability of theoretical perspectives, there is always a chance that one might be admissible which is conducive to theism. When any metaphysics takes itself as the only possible perspective—and even worse, when it does not think of itself as a metaphysics and denies metaphysics as an enterprise—then the situation is serious where God is concerned.

There are signs that such a monolithic view of metaphysics is breaking up today. Kant wanted to restrict metaphysics in the hope of achieving certainty, but such certainty no longer seems to be an obsessive goal among natural scientists. Once certainty is given up as a false hope, there is no need to prohibit metaphysics on the grounds of a supposed failure to produce certainty. Of course, the return to metaphysics by no means in itself assures the production of views which will be as conducive to theism as the recent past was to atheism. What we must first understand is why the climate of the past few centuries so much favored atheism, and then attempt to see what kind of metaphysics theism requires. What kind of first principles are conducive to atheism, what kind are congenial to theism, and which lead to what views of God?

Perhaps it is most important to consider philosophical "rationalism" first. Until the rise of rationalism which we connect with the time of Descartes, philosophy and theology were much more closely united. The split between philosophy and theology, which gradually grew deeper, needs to be examined as one of the roots of contemporary atheism, and this factor is present in Luther's thought too. At first glance this may seem strange, because all the early rationalists—Descartes, Spinoza, and Leibnitz—were theologically inclined. Much as they talk about the separation of philosophy and theology, God plays a large if not decisive role in the thought of these men. Each argues to the existence of God on the basis of a necessary logical conclusion, although the God of each is different. Theology at this same time began, on its Protestant side, to be antiphilosophical, and on its Catholic side to be linked to a philosophy of a special kind. Thus, just as philosophy came to discover that God was not a necessary logical conclusion, the antiphilosophical side of theology rapidly lost its ability to think about God in technical terms, while traditional and scholastic theology tended to identify itself with a particular view of God.

Here are three theistic tendencies which eventually favor atheism: 1) Rationalism considers God in isolation from theology and at first appears philosophically to arrive independently at a description of God and a proof for his existence. As rationalism itself loses its grip on philosophy, however, there appears to be no necessity for reason to lead to God. Now divorced from any association with theology, philosophy no longer draws its thinking about this question from the accumulated theological tradition. The God argued to in philosophy is of a special type. When this ceases to be a necessary conclusion of reason itself, philosophy is not always in a position to generate new concepts of God simply on its own, or at least any that possess vitality.

2. Theology, as it divorces itself from the philosophical movement and preserves only certain views of God, becomes "unphilosophical" in the sense that it begins to take a certain tradition for granted and to allow it a certain exclusive right as a method. Genuine philosophy involves a questioning of the method itself, and it takes no procedure for granted. When this spirit is broken, philosophy is unable to help theology revitalize its concept of God or to aid it in the production of new views.

When the concept of God must be accepted only as it was once formulated, this becomes less and less vital, and the tradition which was preserved is no longer able to sustain itself. Next, the concept of God loses its hold and tends to atheism.

3. In a Protestant setting, if we reject the influence of philosophy, this leaves us with the theological view of God inherited at the time of our separation. Without philosophy's aid, the problem is not the rigid crystallizing of one tradition but the inability to work with the idea of God philosophically at all. This is all right as long as the idea of God present in the theology is acceptable, but when a shift is necessary, the philosophical means to accomplish it are no longer there. In the case above, we observed the effects of a rigidified metaphysics, but in this case the problem is the absence of any. Because the concept of God tends to become inadequate whenever Protestants reject the philosophical tools needed to vitalize it, what once was theism turns to atheism. Men become unable to believe in the God offered to them, and they lack the ability to formulate a new concept.

The rationalism of modern philosophy, at first apparently so congenial to theology, has an a-theistic effect as its reasonings are discovered to be neither necessary nor the only forms. Just as it is cut off from theological connection when reason loses its conviction about necessity, it also seems to reject all Gods if it cannot have one as a necessity of reason. Other philosophical views arise, and empiricism finds that its assumptions need not involve God at all. In fact, in any demand for the immediate confirmation of every theory, the case is loaded against God, and belief in or even discussion of his existence is made very difficult. Empiricism as a philosophical theory is not conducive to the construction of theories about God. Thus, if we are restricted to rather cut-and-dried concepts of God, and are no longer able by temperament to refine them very much, the drift will be toward atheism.

If you do not like any given theory about God, there are two things you can do. You can begin positive reformulation to attempt to find a more adequate theory, or you can enter upon a negative criticism of the view objected to. We will understand our ideological situation in the twentieth century when we un-

103

derstand why most contemporary thought has preferred negative criticism. If the views of God are not adequate to the time, negative criticism has a natural tendency to lead to atheism. This is true because only the more difficult aspects are likely to be pointed out, and the only effective positive answer would be the formulation of a more adequate theory. Has atheism been favored because we have tended more toward negative criticism than to the positive reconstruction of new concepts?

Why is metaphysics so crucial to theological construction that its rejection leads to atheism? Let us take Kant's "moral argument" for God as an example. Kant limits metaphysics and makes it unavailable for theological construction, but he finds that man's moral life requires God. This would seem to establish God without the aid of metaphysics, but the question is not quite so simple. Any argument for God from the moral life must lead to one view of God or another. It would appear that Kant takes the nature of God for granted, but this will not be satisfactory for very long. Let us say that one accepts the argument for God's existence as an implication drawn from some phenomenon in the moral life (e.g., the need for ultimate justice). As soon as you arrive at such a conclusion, your conviction will hold only if the view of God arrived at is expandable and credible.

Any argument can lead to only one aspect of God, and then immediately the question arises about God's other attributes. Thus, conviction is sustained only if the view of God arrived at can be expanded to meet the questions and objections that naturally arise. Unfortunately this is a matter of the metaphysical expansion of the concept, and that cannot be done on the basis of the moral life alone, but only if the necessary basic principles have been clearly worked out.

Can we convince anyone that metaphysics should be allowed again, in order not to restrict theology to what have become inflexible concepts and thus invite atheism? We might list what kinds of metaphysical views seem to favor atheism and what types are conducive to theism and why. This does not establish any one metaphysical view, or even answer the restriction against all metaphysics whatsoever. But if we can sketch this pattern, we might at least be aware of what forces are operating where God is concerned. No one needs to be a theist, but certainly it is too bad if, being interested in theism, you adopt a basic set of assumptions which actually give the favorable odds to atheism.

To recapitulate some of what we have discovered, the following views about metaphysics seem conducive to atheism, although it is possible that in different eras, when their assumptions were more widely spread, they actually had the opposite effect.

1. First, of course, is any antiphilosophical or antimetaphysical attitude itself. When metaphysics is cut off, we lose our ability to speak about God systematically, since this is an acquired ability and not inborn. When metaphysics is outlawed, we do not have to face the challenge of alternative views which are not theistic, but we also restrict theology only to those views of God which are either current or past.

2. Perhaps the next most important antitheistic factor is the assumption that a metaphysics which was once conducive to theism will necessarily always be so. To say this is not to assume some neat view of the linear evolution of theory, since it can be the case that some earlier metaphysical view (perhaps with alterations) may still be adequate as a theological base. It is just that this is not necessarily so, and cannot be assumed without risking atheism if the once accepted metaphysics is no longer taken for granted. Any theistic view, then, which welds itself to any one metaphysical framework, however attractive at any given time, is risking atheism as the metaphysical perspective comes to need basic rethinking and its exclusive attachment makes this impossible. Metaphysical views are not forged by an attempt to hold tightly to a given theoretical structure, and it is hard to see how they can be preserved in this way.

3. Theology has often feared philosophy in general or some metaphysics in particular. Thus, it has tended to withdraw defensively when any view claims a privileged truth for itself to the exclusion of all other theories. Yet, too complete a separation leads to atheism, since theology cannot elaborate the metaphysical base it needs to speak about God. The right way out of this is to oppose all exclusiveness in metaphysics, to reject necessity

as inhering in any one view, to elaborate alternatives to the metaphysics offered, and then to establish the right to use some different framework in which to expand a theory of the divine attributes.

4. Extreme rationalism may seem temporarily to yield a God as a result of its reasoning, but in a time more impressed with a variety of possibilities than with some one necessity—and in an age well aware of the violence of counterrational forces—a strict rationalism will tend toward atheism as its rigidity is rejected. It is only for theism that rationalism seems a dangerous basis today. In a humanistic view, we can recognize the variability of perspectives around us and the existence of counterrational forces, and these do not disturb us. We know that the whole world does not share our rationalism, and as humanists we can still call men to join us in this endeavor to establish reason as our guide. Transferred to theology, however, this metaphysics is subversive, since God must account for all men and all forces in the world and not just the reason of the humanists. If it fails to provide this world-wide scope, an exclusive rationalistic metaphysics in theology tends to atheism as its lack of comprehensive explanation becomes clear.

5. Romanticism is also a good example of an outlook which may lead to atheism eventually. To think of men as basically good, to exalt nature as fundamentally all good, or to see human nature as tending to produce beauties from itself naturally, to exalt the powers of creativity in man—any view like this which fails to come to grips which the negative, destructive, and degenerate forces will tend to atheism as the well-known romantic cycle of disillusion appears. Any given individual may succeed in building around himself a romantic picture of man and the aspects of the world which he selects. But what may lead individually to a romantic and consoling deity, when used as a general metaphysical outlook for theology is bound to tend to atheism, as we discover that all the world's forces and all the world's men are not accounted for by such an optimistic outlook. In another day romanticism was more possible, when we took the world we occupy for granted and as necessary. Now we see ourselves in a world far more dismal than some which are and

were possible, and romanticism is unable to produce a God who can explain his less-than-romantic choice. Waste and destruction are too apparent, and we have lost our romanticism about the natural development of a golden era yet to come.

6. Empiricism has been strong for centuries, and as a view which is based on immediacies and the possibility for a definitive check on disagreements by an appeal to a concrete base, it offers a strong alternative for those who would like to settle matters clearly and on the basis of immediate evidence. Without calling into question at the moment the kind of view of the world's structure which an empiricism may assume, its aversion to hidden and nonsurface qualities makes it immediately difficult for theology. From the surface of the world a satisfactory God simply cannot be extracted, or at least not one who is very adequate in his ability to explain a difficult world. A God constructed on an empirical base will tend to be rejected, just as Hume illustrated in his analysis of "natural religion." The demand for immediate confirmation (which usually accompanies empiricism) itself tends to atheism, since God is not subject to such procedures. Nothing has ever prevented any one from following empiricism, and it probably will always have a certain appeal, but theologically it is a prime factor in the atheistic temper of recent times.

7. Nonmetaphysical arguments, e.g., from the moral life or based on aesthetic or religious experience, etc., all tend to atheism if they cannot construct and defend an adequate theory of God, or if they allow their arguments to lead to some preconceived notion of God that is accepted without reconstruction. In general, any argument for God based on other phenomena may or may not eventually tend to atheism. That depends on how adequate the view of God is, once it is arrived at. Anselm's famous argument brings many men to understand "God" in each new day, but it does not keep them there if the concept of God offered is not sufficiently elaborate or acceptable to hold them. If combined with metaphysical elaboration, any moral or religious argument may establish a God, but then it is the vitality of the view of God offered that holds an argument to theism when otherwise it might tend to atheism. This happens if the

107

concept of God arrived at is insufficient to support belief and to answer the inevitable myriad negative questions that arise once you succeed in bringing God into view.

8. Existentialism too, at least in its origin as we have pointed out, falls into the class of nonmetaphysical arguments which lead to God but which then often lapse into atheism, because the antimetaphysical attitude associated with it cannot produce a view of God consistent with that theory's novelties. However, there are certain additional factors about existentialism, in addition to its widespread contemporary influence, which make it atheistic in its thrust in spite of God's prominence and its original religious context. In addition to the fact that existentialism seems incapable of producing a view of God commensurate with or sufficient in detail to support its profundities, its technical use of such concepts as "the individual," "subjectivity," and "the moment" tend to work against theism. Without exploring these concepts in detail as they are used, say, by Kierkegaard, what ought to be noted is that such concepts need not be atheistic in thought. It is just that they can become so unless they are complemented by a detailed discussion of exactly how they apply to God.

The psychological explorations of "the moment" and its significance for the individual in his subjective choice, for instance —all this works against theism only if the concept is at odds with one's view of God's nature, which it actually tends to be for Kierkegaard. If "the moment" could be analyzed in detail as to its application to God, a revised concept of God might emerge rather than the rejection of an inharmonious God. This, of course, would mean redoing quite radically some traditional views of God's relation to time, but this is metaphysical analysis which Kierkegaard will not engage in. In order to support theism very long, the central categories develop in any philosophical analysis must be given a foundation in the divine nature, since to do this is the very business of theology. Existentialism illustrates, then, the atheistic drive of any view which cannot revamp (with some novelty) its concept of God in the light of the central concepts it has developed elsewhere.

Now, considering the metaphysics of atheism, it is time to ask what views, then, are conducive to theism. The answer to this is simple; it is not very detailed, but that is consistent with the theme of this essay as an attempt to find a view of God in negativity. If you are interested in a revitalized theism, you must begin by accepting the necessity for metaphysics, although never one form to the exclusion of all others. Then, studying the qualities of those metaphysical views which tend to atheism, you must work out a metaphysical frame with these forces in mind. You should not avoid all these views absolutely, but simply move in awareness of the forces within them that work against theism. Radical novelty or discontinuity in metaphysical terminology ought to be avoided or at least approached cautiously. This means that traditional views can form the starting point, if amended and altered by a knowledge of what changes have taken place, and this is done in the light of what you wish to accomplish theologically. As you see the metaphysics develop and the view of God emerge in the writing of any earlier author, you gain sensitivity as to what factors carry what consequences —e.g., that a stress upon necessity either makes freedom impossible or at least alters its meaning radically.

Just as we can see how certain metaphysical views tend to atheism unless altered and forcefully molded into a new form, so you can see what kind of God will tend to result from what kind of metaphysical assumptions. When you see what view of God each assumed first principle leads to, you can elaborate a theory with one eye on the theological objectives (e.g., freedom or an explanation of evil) and another eye on how the first principles you are operating with tend to lead toward or away from such goals. Any completed theology will be the result of the controlled interplay of these forces as they are now molded and given form by the philosopher-theologian. To attempt theology without a sensitivity to the directional tendencies of the metaphysics employed is either to reach God blindly and by accident or to invite a powerless drift toward atheism. The wages of metaphysical stupidity are atheism.

CHAPTER IX

The Difficulties of Remaining in Atheism

Your hideous face
composed of lust and filth and gibberish
sweeps all doubts away—all. Since
the devil exists, God also exists.
Otherwise *you* would have won a long time ago.

> RECARDO, in Rolf Hochhuth's *The Deputy*, as he confronts the German exterminator of the Jews.

In attempting to trace the obviously powerful sources of atheism which always operate but which have been particularly strong in recent centuries, at some point we should turn and attempt to explain why atheism has not long ago quietly proclaimed victory and sealed the issue. The fact that this has not happened, and the fact that organized religion (if not theism) has shown renewed vitality of late—these factors must indicate that the active forces do not all move in one direction. Some factors continually move toward theism as well as toward atheism, even if not with equal power.

Any negative argument, when it is as forceful as the reason leading to atheism, tends toward a negative conclusion. Just as atheism gains its power because the view of God offered appears oversimplified and unable to account for certain forces of violence, so when any simple positive view of God is rejected it becomes apparent that not everything is accounted for by denial either. In the vacuum left by the rejection of some one view of God, a natural tendency develops to move back again to test other possible positive assumptions. As indicated previously, the rejection of one untenable theory of the divine nature does not take care of the perhaps infinite other possible views. The forces of atheism often have this interesting effect: after they have swept away one view of God, they open the field for thought so that other possible Gods may be suggested to us.

In a world that is not all negative, it is hard to hold yourself to a purely negative conclusion, since that does not exactly correspond to the facts of life. In terms of the statement from *The Deputy* quoted above, the first impact of a powerful malignant force leads to a denial of God, but its second impact can be the consideration of what it is that holds evil in check so that its destruction and betrayal, though extensive, at least are not complete. When the Devil appears and the force of evil makes God disappear, the fact that we are not utterly destroyed can make us turn back again to consider the power and force of life. Then, perhaps, we can discover a view of God tempered by a prior encounter with negativity.

We often reject God in order to explain the presence of destructive powers. That being done, we are faced with the need to explain why and how we are able to resist the total subversion of life by evil. Having given the Devil his due, how can we explain what he cannot explain, if we grant that we first introduced the Devil to explain what a simple, good God could not account for? It is a fact that all is not evil or wastefully destructive—just as it is a fact that not all can be called good and pleasant and positive by any stretch of the imagination.

It is difficult to remain in atheism because removing God still leaves unexplained those same factors which the view of God could not adequately account for. Then it becomes apparent that what was rejected was not an explanation of all the forces in life, whether good or evil, but simply an inadequate explanation. If we could give up the attempt to explain the reasons why our world is constituted as it is, perhaps it might be possible to remain in atheism. If we cannot, atheism often simply sets in motion a countersearch for a more adequate explanation. We must begin, of course, with an attempt to define what "adequate" will mean, since that is where atheism got its start, i.e., by rejecting as "not adequate" what some accept.

Atheism is the most difficult of all positions to be in if one wishes to avoid the search for God, since it is impossible to rest content until you can be sure there are no more dragons left, i.e., no more possible concepts of God. Yet it is impossible for a man to live to eternity, so as to go through the whole sequence. You must be sure, after denying the existence of one concept, that none can exist beside the one you have just rejected. As a matter of fact, it is hard to conceive how a new concept of God could be formed, except by the at least partial rejection of some existing view as inadequate; so that this tendency itself is the means by which a new idea is formed. Arriving in atheism, one is next haunted by the absence of God and by the possibility that some as yet unexplored concept of God remains, or that one may in fact exist, i.e., some future experience may lead to a being who corresponds to the concept.

We cannot escape the fact that the world might have been all evil, without even small areas of individual meaning. It might have been both incapable of holding itself together and unable to produce life; but the fact is that it is a self-sustaining universe within which life is possible. Even at its worst, it still has a minimum of meaning and value. If we reject one theory of origin or one view of how the world came to be and for what purpose, the unavoidable fact is that it did come to be and that it moves as a self-contained organic whole to produce life.

The existence of negative and destructive forces, however severe, being granted, at least they were not sufficient to prevent the world from taking form, nor are they powerful enough to stop life altogether. They might have been, but the fact that they were not powerful enough to block all creation itself requires some explanation. Granting the range of destruction present, what held these forces in check in creation? What power formed a world in spite of all resistance, and still holds evil in check against total annihilation? Attempting to explain the limits and

112

restraints set on evil and on all destructive forces, once this power has led to atheism, may lead to the consideration of a new view of God.

We take the form of the universe to be neither necessary nor the only possible one. This being true, something must explain how we got just the combination we have in spite of its manifest deficiencies. Why was the line drawn just at this point and not another? Why do the forces of destruction and malignancy have just the range they do; why are they neither greater nor less in power? In itself evil knows no limits in its destruction of life, just as goodness tends to communicate itself without limit at the other extreme. Destruction continues until nothing is left, unless checked from outside itself. The limits set upon evil can only come from something other than itself, and what kind of being is capable of holding evil in order to a set limit?

Earlier we discussed the fact that God's nonevidence leads to the idea of a God in hiding, which in itself gives credence to atheism. It is also true that a hidden God often simply incites an attempt to find him. After failure, as long as life lasts there is a tendency to try again, and this renewed vitality makes it difficult to rest in atheism. Or, sometimes we deny a God who is too easy to refute, and again our sporting blood rebels. Left with a guilty conscience, like a bully who picks only on little children, we realize that we have induced atheism by attacking a naïve concept of God. This may offend our sense of fairness, and we keep wondering what an adequate God might be like.

Determined not to win by picking out only vulnerable, unmoving targets, we naturally come to think that there must be a concept of God more resistant than one which falls merely because it was too weak to begin with. *The search for a more vigorous concept of God in itself leads away from atheism, and it may just as well lead to a new God as back to atheism once more.* That is the argument for God from the existence of the Devil. As long as life lasts, the discovery of an adequate concept of God is always a possibility, and this is a realization which perhaps only our arrival at atheism can bring to us.

We have pointed out that, just as concepts about God, if left alone, tend to fade and die, so also does atheism, since it depends

113

for its conviction on the firmness of the concept of God it denies. The idea of God that atheism opposes so vigorously will tend in due course to weaken, and so—somewhat ironically—the force of atheism will fade with it. This tendency of views of God to lose their force also applies to the atheism that results from the denial of any one of them. Thus, one may become an atheist under the propulsion of powerful forces, but these forces in turn also tend to fade, and then they operate to undercut atheism.

In discussing the idea of the "death of God," we suggested that this might be given a strong traditional meaning by considering it as the issue of whether God suffered death himself on Golgotha in the person of Jesus. If we lack an idea of God capable of accepting into itself this assertion, God tends to die in the face of our acceptance of the forces of death all around us. However, if we could construct an idea of God such that he would be capable of receiving death into himself, he might also explain in himself why atheism is possible. He would be capable of descending to death, and that is the very point at which atheism often begins.

A God who cannot accept death encourages atheism, or at least he does so at the moment of disappearance, just as the disciples scattered, broken and disillusioned, when Jesus was taken down from the cross. How such a view of God might lead from this natural point of atheism to some new theism depends on working out in detail how God can be said to die. This is something which Christians have asserted traditionally, but they have seldom worked it out in technical detail. Beginning at the point of death, however, a more adequate concept of God might be formed on this apparently negative basis.

In analyzing the forces of atheism, we first suggested that the odds actually favor it. When religious belief once dominated all thought, to assert atheism seemed like backing a bold cause and championing freedom and the underdog. Now that a tendency to atheism actually dominates the intellectual scene, the very fact that the odds are against any theism in itself might move some away from atheism when they discover that now they are on the side of an easy new orthodoxy. Now the hard way is to search to see whether there is not some still unexplored and

114

more potent idea of God which can be uncovered and elaborated.

The amazing phenomenon of our day—that religious faith can remain while an explicit God is denied—this suggests the need to search for a God who is equal to such faith. Religious conviction does not disappear even when the God on whom it depends becomes vague and imprecise. This suggests that the reason why God has disappeared in the first place is that the view of God offered was not equal to the religious assertions. When atheism is reached, and when any given view of God is rejected, if religion as a phenomenon also died it would be easy to remain in atheism. Of course sentiment, superstition, etc., may account for religion lingering on as a practice after God is no longer believed in. Still, religion would at least tend to disappear after a time rather than to sustain itself—that is, if it were not continually renewed by the search for a concept of God equal to itself. The good actions of a church or of any religious body keep alive a religious practice even when no clear notion of God remains to support it. This keeps open the suggestion that perhaps the atheist should try again. He is challenged to see if there isn't a God sufficient to match a continued religious devotion and selfless service. Atheism is always made restless by its inability to put an end to religious vitality. It ought to die but it doesn't.

If religious faith is left without an adequate God, it may tend to escalate toward mysticism. If in turn this tends to atheism, such a process may suggest a new search for a God equal to the belief. If so, where should we start? Despite all the dangers of mysticism I have pointed out, perhaps it also offers an answer to this question. We should begin to look precisely at the point where God disappeared. Once a tradition has been broken, if you can intersect it again at the point where it was last known to be powerful, perhaps it may move forward to a new concept of God, beginning from the exact point at which the decline began. Mysticism claims to discover God where a former inadequate God disappears, but often this new God is beyond speech. If God disappears under the various internal and external pressures which lead toward atheism, then, at the exact point of that disappearance, a fresh thread of development may be uncovered.

It would begin by developing a new thought out from that point rather than maintaining a mystical silence. Such a possibility of speaking about God again makes remaining in atheism a restless affair. "Since the Devil exists, God also exists."

In this ch. he arrives at her thesis — rather, evil does not acct fr all reality — ∴ perhaps we ought to consider optional views of God

why is hard to talk to Kingdom of God

CHAPTER X

The Insights of the Vulgar

If we wish to start from the arguments against God and attempt to construct a theory about God in the light of these, where is the material to come from? In more aristocratically oriented days, our examples came from kings and noble men. God seemed to be—for St. Anselm for example—"a being than which none greater can be conceived," and this description emphasizes the tendency to see Being in hierarchies with God at the top. Such a way of conceiving of God is majestic, and certainly, if he is to be the responsible creator of this vast complex which we see, he must be powerful and second to none in rank. Nevertheless, however fruitful it once was to conceive of Being in hierarchies with God at the pinnacle, this avenue no longer seems convincing. Democracy, which has been spreading for several centuries, has had a leveling effect which extends even to God. We are, for better or for worse, in the era of the vulgar. The common man is now our hero and not the royal prince. Whatever God's aristocratic attributes may once have been, to attempt to conceive of him in this way now is to invite atheism.

How is it possible to conceive of God on the level of the vulgar, and why is this now necessary? If theodicy—i.e., the demand to explain why evil was given such a powerful hand when it might have been curbed—is a primary force driving us toward atheism today, this question also puts its greatest stress

117

on the ordinary man and not on the king. Tragedy once took as its theme the suffering of kings. We do know that the highborn and the powerful actually suffer. The difficulty is that their suffering seems neither to affect God nor to help those of us who deal with our fate in the midst of other circumstances. Theirs is a royal drama, and it takes place in a life filled with meaning, significance, and nobility. Observing such suffering does not break us; rather, we are edified by it. God may purify a strong soul through suffering in this way without arousing our anger. However, today our heroes have changed. When the lonely and the downtrodden are central in our focus, it is much more difficult to justify their suffering or reconcile it with a sensitive God. Suffering in the midst of a meaningless and drab existence is more difficult to accept than a God who tests only strong and powerful men in the midst of royal splendor.

If a shift in focus away from nobility and toward the vulgar only increases our difficulty with the problem of evil, a kingly God may now be out of place, and his incongruous presence can become a cause for atheism in a vulgar era. Any attempt to construct a theory of God with atheism as its impetus, then, will have to use a new sort of material. How can the vulgar instruct us as to what God might be like? When in past centuries our thoughts were ordered toward royalty, the misery of the masses did not seem so out of place. However, when we worry more about men without distinction or position, then the suffering and cruelty present in the world assume staggering proportions. As long as the least supported the best, we could judge God by the highest achievement and not by the average condition. Now that we see how miserable a majority have been and still are, any view of God drawn on this basis will have to be considerably different from a vision of royal splendor.

Arthur Miller's *Death of a Salesman* is a classic of our time. Here we see a poor man with thoughts that exceed his accomplishments. He is caught in lies and is slowly going down. He is the victim of his situation, one for which his feeble talents are no match. He is not a noble figure. John Steinbeck's *Tortilla Flat* portrays even humbler figures who eat, steal, argue, and get drunk. Tennessee William's characters are often "low-class," and William Faulkner's *Requiem for a Nun* certainly does not celebrate a traditionally saintly person. In literature we have recently explored and gained our lessons from the common and the cheap rather than from the aristocratic (just as contemporary metaphysics starts with nonbeing rather than being). When such material as this forms the basis for our insights, a kingly God is so far removed as to become nonexistent. Yet what kind of God might such a new center of attention result in? If we use this as a context in which to develop a modern concept of God, would this solve the problem of evil or simply make it more intense?

It would seem that any acceptable God today would have to be a "people's God." He should not be completely above them in kind in the way that the powerful and successful are. The good and the true and the beautiful are no longer sufficient to lead us to a God, since no majority are ever like this. The masses suffer and spark violence, and any God who could create them or who is able to attract their devotion cannot be wholly removed from such action. A God of absolute tranquillity and rest explains only a small portion—although admittedly a valuable portion—so that he cannot be the God of the vulgar. Our problem is this: To what kind of God are suffering and violence not alien? If the violence of the world is to find a correspondence in his nature, what can be its place in God's life if it is so common among men? We are no longer allowed to dismiss unpleasant features as merely lesser goods, but instead we must look to the struggles of the poorly educated for our insight.

If God is to be vulgarized too, we might actually learn more from the vast common tide which seems to be set against a highborn God. Not that every common man is against God or every aristocrat for him. The breakdown is not that simple. In fact God often seems less real today in noble circles then in ordinary surroundings. If it is true that in the past common men were elevated merely by following this royal example, a God drawn on common principles would at first glance seem not to be a very elevating figure, but that is a question still to be explored. Does such a leveling process necessarily produce a mediocre God, since this is sometimes the result of a revolt against aristocracy? Why did God not create a world of fewer people of higher quality? A small aristocracy, with just an adequate servant class, would seem to have much to recommend it. What kind of God would ignore this pleasant option?

"The simple" will perhaps be our keynote here. The world is a very complex place, and thus any understanding of it must also be to a certain extent complex. Any attempt to take in all the events of the world as a whole runs into complexities beyond the mind's ability to absorb. Yet, it is a common experience that insight comes in very simple formulae. As long as the mind moves upward to ever greater complexity and sophistication, thre is no guarantee of insight, and we often fall victim to the weight of an inherited or a self-generated mass of detail which is too involved to be absorbed. What can produce a simple formula of power around which the mind may orient its mass of facts?

The vulgar can be instructive here, for our mind needs constantly to be reduced to elementary terms. The royal and the noble allow us to ignore the fundamentals of existence, but the poor and the world's failures do not allow us to turn away from basic facts. To purge the mind of the artificial and its acquired intricacies always produces anguish. The suffering involved in living through such a stripping away of luxury makes possible the production of a very simple statement. Our mind moves away from simplicity naturally, and when it does its vision is blocked until it can shed its complexity and summarize simply again. The revolution of the masses destroys cumbersome complexities and reduces us to simplicities. This may be the only situation from which God can be discovered again, i.e., in the midst of the rubble, after the riot, when our energies are exhausted.

Of course, if God is vastly different in kind from ourselves, such an approach will only lead us in the wrong direction. The technical issue of the "univocity of being" (whether all Being at its core has common attributes) is involved here. If God is a very exalted figure, perhaps even radically different in kind from us, we should distill out the most noble and the most exalted aspects of the world and men as Anselm sought to do. Then we could use these as a basis of comparison in order to project ourselves beyond the ordinary level of our existence. In general, this has

120

been the procedure in theology since Plato objected to attributing human faults to the Greek gods and asserted that they were responsible only for the good.

If we now set out to derive our insight from the vulgar, what we are presupposing is that God is not a being radically different in kind from us, nor can he be beyond Being as Tillich thought. This does not mean that we must go to the opposite extreme—i.e., attributing mud and hair to eternal things, which worried Plato. What it does mean is that, present somewhere within the common and the ordinary, there is a simple insight to be discovered, and the question is how to strip life down to that core. Not that it can be found blantantly spread across the surface of the world's poor. But only a study of the vulgar can produce the simplicity our intellect needs and cause the simple, common attributes to rise to the surface for us to grasp. Perhaps in the unsettling consequences of a leveling process God can be found today. It is here that the elements of life are, sometimes brutally, revealed.

In what sense are the forces of atheism instructive at this point? Perhaps chief among the many factors contributing to our widespread atheism is the problem of evil, and as we noted above, a concentration on the vulgar only heightens this difficulty. Evil, among the rich lives of the royally born, is not as difficult to reconcile with God as is mass misery in the midst of meaninglessness. A radically transcendent God does not seem to meet this issue either, except perhaps to take the minds of some few off the problem by drawing them away from it. If study of the vulgar is capable of producing insight, a God constructed on this model will have to be more closely identified in his nature with the area where the problem of evil is most severe.

The concept of the "univocity of Being" never did mean that God and man are identical in nature. It simply asserts that a common core or nature can be found, and that such a basis of understanding does not transcend man's grasp but actually forms the core of his normal mode of knowledge. If in the tragedies of the simple and the unsuccessful the insight into Being can now be found, and if a view of God is then constructed from this, it can only be a univocal concept if it is erected on this vulgar base.

121

There must be a common point of identity between man and God in suffering, or the problem of evil could not be dealt with by such a new view of God. As democracy has discovered, attention to the vulgar involves a leveling process so extreme that even God and man discover a common core.

What a concentration upon the vulgar as our example tells us is that any God not immediately identified with the lowest side of man, as well as with his noblest side, will tend to be rejected. In spite of elaborate and complex surface differences, all Being is to be understood through common attributes discovered at its core, God included. In classical drama, the suffering of the noble lifted us because of the meaning it lent to suffering. In this sense it provided an answer to the problem of evil. We were edified, if not purified, in following the struggles of the gifted. Their language was exalted and their position in itself lent meaning and dignity to any human struggle. That they should so nobly bear adversity made it easier, by participation, for those less fortunate to do so too. Now our question is: Does the suffering of the unfortunate degrade us so that we are torn down rather than uplifted?

The language of Faulkner and Steinbeck borders on the primitive, and Tennessee Williams presents scenes which polite people do not enact. On the other hand, if we really do learn important insights from Arthur Miller's unfortunate figures, what is the nature of the insight and what does it tell us? It does seem to point down rather than up, which means that its first effect is to drag us further down instead of lifting us. Most of those who read this literature do not live on as primitive or elemental a level as the characters portrayed. We experience vicariously emotions which often are more base than our own, rather than the exalted thought of the fortunate and highborn. What kind of insight is this, and what can it tell us about an acceptable view of God?

Suffering which is nobly born and a kingly God—these go very well together. It is not hard to identify with a king in his trials. The broken suffering of the less powerful will have to be instructive in some other way. The first thing to be noted is that such harsh experience tends to strip away pretense; it treats lightly the

122

elaborately created cultural achievements of man. Good manners protect man from unpleasant facts, but this modern form of literature tends to ignore manners and to leave us helpless. We are reduced and exposed to the raw forces in life, and it must be in this sense that what is vulgar can be instructive, if at all.

Granted that it is possible to see how an approach through the vulgar can be illuminating in this sense, i.e., by laying bare the elemental forces in life, how can it help in forming a concept of God? In the first place, we discover that evil is not really fully explained in noble suffering. The well-born and the well-endowed are of sufficient quality either to bear it or to break under it at least with tragic significance. Evil is at its most perplexing when it strikes those whose powers and situation make them unequal to cope with its brutal force. Thus, if a vulgar image leads us to a concept of God, it could be to one constructed on a plane adequate to explain evil at its most perplexing level. Such a God adds meaning by lowering himself and not by being exalted. He is discovered in the midst of the low points of life as well as at its heights.

A God drawn on this basis will be different. How? At least the God who arises in this new way will not be estranged from the basic features of human existence, since a raw human nature afflicted by evil first gave us our clue to him. Being will be one, and since it is undivided it will not be so difficult to account for its lowest reaches. However, if we are given a univocal concept, the problem is to derive a God sufficiently exalted to fulfill his office, e.g., to be powerful and intelligent enough to create the universe from himself. Today, of course, nothing seems to exceed our reason, least of all infinites, so that a God derived from the insights of the vulgar might perfectly well be infinite in power, as opposed to man's more limited scope. This is not incompatible with what we learn when we take common men as our heroes. Their limitations are their downfall, and thus God, in order not to fail too, must be seen as without limits to his power.

The similarities between God and men come in at other points than power: a participation in suffering, a knowledge of the responsibility for decisions, a facing of contingency, the accep-

123

tance of possibility, the lack of necessity, and the enjoyment of simple pleasures and common events. Such a picture of God can be drawn, and it does not lack some classical elements of perfection, although it is radically altered in its conception in other ways. If we must sink to the lowest possible level as the only way to achieve an insight into Being, "emotion" will not be missing there. Instead, it will be central to the divine life itself. To be swayed by emotion is not in itself bad. Everything depends on how emotion is controlled, and now we may begin to see the difference between God and man, although this comes only after having first discovered their basic identity. God's emotions are infinitely stronger than ours; the difference is that he can always keep them in his control.

Violence and suffering were once thought to be, above all else, inapplicable to God. How can what were once considered central imperfections now become perfections in a new idea of God? "To suffer" for Spinoza meant to pass to a lower level of existence, and both for man and for God this was to be avoided at all costs. To suffer also indicated a subordination to another being, whose level of being rose as the existence of those who suffered fell. Violence tears any particular being apart. Since this seemed to happen only to the inferior, it was therefore to be excluded from any God conceived of as perfect. This was the classical line of argument.

If the vulgar are to provide our insights, our idea of what is "perfect" must be changed. This much seems clear: to absorb violence will no longer be bad; in fact it will be necessary. Without it no depths can be reached and no unnecessary complications shaken off. Violence alone is able to bring the elements of Being to light. Men are purified by it but also sometimes twisted and destroyed. God is purified by it, but he sustains himself intact, since his power is equal to any force. If God succeeds where men fail, he is similar to them in existence, but will his example be relevant to man's plight?

"Suffering" is perhaps an even more central concept here, that is, if the vulgar are to be our teachers. To suffer means to pass to a lower stage of being; but if God has now lost his pride, there is no harm in undergoing this if he loses neither his being nor his control. Suffering may overpower and break a man, but God is sufficient to sustain himself under its pressure. Passage to a lower stage is itself a revelation of being, but only if you do not fall apart in the process. God is able to sustain himself at being's lowest and most degraded depths; he can resist these erosions. He still remains a God in control even when he is pushed toward dissolution.

To suffer and to pass to a lower mode of being reveals man's nature, and the fact that God can himself enter into this experience uncovers perhaps the central feature of his nature too. Although the effects of pressure on man and God may be different, their univocal being becomes most evident in their passage through common suffering. God can master this, and man must learn to do so or be destroyed. The relevance of God to the common man's plight lies in the application of the same forces to God that the vulgar must endure; the difference lies in their ability to cope with these forces successfully.

If we attempt to capitalize on the insights of the vulgar for theological purposes, we must point out carefully that others in earlier ages have already written about the common people as heroes. What is new about this is that in a recent generation we have turned even more in this direction; we have assumed that we can find here not only minor insights but also a penetration into the structure of Being itself. Now it is here that you must seek even God. The use of vulgar insights has previously not really been taken as theological material, however interesting it was for literature and drama. In fact, the tendency has been almost the reverse, i.e., to exclude the ill-mannered and form a ladder of nobility from which to draw our concept of God by projection upward from the highest and the best that is known. It is also true that, in some earlier uses of common people, their simplicity was highly romanticized. A brief glance at Miller, Steinbeck, Faulkner, and Williams will indicate that our use of the vulgar is now rough and harsh and not at all a romantic idealization of their supposed simplicity.

The issue concerns our starting point and its effect on our final concept of God. If we claim what is common as the basis for insight, this is particularly unusual when the subject is God. This is more revolutionary as a theological method than it might at first appear, since classically the method has been to eliminate the lower as being inapplicable to God and as inappropriate to his perfection. Now no attribute is to be eliminated as inappropriate, although that is not the end of the matter theologically (i.e., to have the mass of all the world's attributes simply attached to God), but it is where we propose to begin our systematic construction. Then, how do we proceed? The answer is that our insight is drawn from the specific, the vulgar, the common, the particular life situation without having the resulting concept remain simply these. How can that be? This avenue can be appropriate and God can himself be vulgar and particular only if he is equally present and equally to be inferred from the lowest as well as the highest. This democracy in the formation of our concept does not eliminate the hierarchy of values. It simply draws its insight equally from all levels and without drawing any class distinctions at the outset. God is no more to be found among the noble than among the vulgar, but among both.

Such a view of God depends on a projection beyond our own mode of being, but first we must find God's univocal meeting point with the peasant's nature. We must find what high and low share alike, and more important, what evil and good both exhibit when taken together. This is why atheism and an argument from the existence of the Devil are the proper place to begin to talk about God in the twentieth century. Otherwise our natural tendency is to reject certain material; we select and orient the concept of God entirely from one end of the spectrum. This is the easiest thing to do and it has an element of elegance, but atheism's force today holds us in check against such an approach to God, which no longer can be as acceptable as it once was. Furthermore, a view of God constructed with only one set of qualities in mind is weak in its power to explain the extent of the whole spectrum, as a study of Plotinus will indicate. It can account for itself and for the best, but its account of the worst is necessarily indirect and weak. This difficulty is more pronounced today, once we no longer accept the evil and the inferior as necessary but work for their elimination instead.

It is neither easy nor automatic to form a concept of God. If

126

it is now to be based on a univocal concept of Being, this is still not easy to discern beneath the world's amazing variety. Evil and violence and destruction, and the despair which results from experiencing Nonbeing—perhaps these negative forces alone possess sufficient power to cause a breakthrough to reveal Being to us. What is clean and pure and all-white (as Plato tells us in the *Philebus*) is pleasant, but—ironically—it does not contain much force to cause one to look beneath a surface. It cannot account for what is unlike it and yet surrounds it and outnumbers it. Of course, God was conceived originally along kingly lines so that he would have a power to rule and control which the common man does not possess. Will this power to create now be lost, and does God become just another man if the vulgar produce our insights into Being?

This does not need to be the result. Immediately after seeing what common aspects God shares with all men and creation, we are then faced with the problem of saying how he differs from man. Using evil and nonbeing now as a positive base and not a negative one, we must attempt to work out how God still differs from the lowest. To work out this theory of the divine nature in detail is a subject for long study, but at least one illustration may be given here: Does God suffer anguish in the experience of Nonbeing? Our answer: Yes. How does this differ, then, from man's experience? God knows the freedom that nothing needs to be as it is, and he suffers in the face of such indeterminacy and Nonbeing. In man such suffering can prevent him from acting or even from assuming any form of being, but God's power is sufficient to guarantee his decision in the face of anguish. Man can succumb through lack of power and knowledge; God has power sufficient to sustain himself in the face of the suffering which Nonbeing induces.

Having begun with the problem of evil, our question is: does such a reconstructed view of God actually solve the problem of evil or does it only make it more intense? In one way, a view of God drawn from the insights of the vulgar does make the problem of evil more severe. On an aristocratic basis, at least those few who achieved noble and beautiful things were in some sense an answer to destruction, and at least you could concentrate on

127

seeing good things as embodied in the best. A democracy, one in which no level is valued more than another, makes such virtuous achievements no longer so impressive as an answer to the problem of evil, precisely because this accounts for so little in the world, and our given base is now so broad. Misery only becomes greater when all of Being is considered on a democratic basis. Our defenses against destruction are now less, and the tools to combat it fewer. In this sense, the problem of evil is intensified, not relieved, since the basis we have elected does not allow us to ignore so much quantity in favor of so little quality.

A God drawn from such material as we propose can deal with the problem of evil only if he is a God more geared by nature to suffering. He must now be capable of identifying with man on this level and powerful enough to have elected this appalling way when nothing necessitated his doing so. The problem of divine perfection is at issue here, for there are good reasons why the theological tradition took its characteristics for God only from the best. The difficulty is that we know the concept of perfection to be variable too,* and so God need not exist in only one mode in order to be perfect. However, can a view drawn on a wider base develop a concept of perfection so that God shares in, yet is not subject to, man's faults? Can God possess the elements of failure and still not actually fail—and if so, in virtue of what capacities is he different from men, so that he suffers from the forces which threaten them and yet is exempt from actual destruction?

The argument from negation at least outlines the issue that must be faced, and if we can set the problem, that is at least half the answer. In this case, what we must prove is in what way a tendency toward descent and leveling can also lift up and purify. Can a God drawn on common principles be elevating as well as companionable? If when the threat of destruction is at its greatest (e.g., death) the structures of Being also become clearest, because they are illuminated by the threat of Nonbeing, *God may also be discerned in the lowest precisely because the core of*

*For a detailed discussion of the variety of concepts of God possible while still being "perfect," see my *Divine Perfection: Possible Ideas of God* (New York: Harper & Row, 1961).

every experience is univocally applicable to God. Only if Being and Nonbeing are related in this way can descent and leveling be illuminating and more basically revelatory than a discriminating selection of the best. On the surface the differences that separate us are wide, so that perhaps only in the stripping away that violence involves can a core of identity be found in Being which unites man and man as well as man and God. In this way the threat of destruction is necessary to any basic insight, or at least to one which hopes to account for all of Being and Nonbeing, good and evil, and not just the better part of existence.

Take, for instance, the elements involved in failure. To fail is often to lack the power needed to accomplish an end. In that sense God does not fail, whereas men can. Yet in a more basic sense, failure involves a loss of being. Observing this deficiency in the vulgar, we may decide what God shares in this core of failure. No being can be without losing some of its being. Nothing that is, needs to be, and so any given entity may always be eliminated at any time by decisive action. In realizing this, men often become needlessly aggressive and destructive, and then they spread failure in their wake. God, when he deals with this situation, makes certain determinations, but he does not surrender control to them in spite of their lack of necessity. Realizing the lack of necessity in the ordained system, men often rebel and alter it. Sometimes they do this with success and sometimes they produce only failure. In any failure of being, God also fails, although we do not yet know what he might do in the future to recoup his failure. To date, however, to observe the destructive powers which are all too present is to observe God's ability to share in contemporary failure.

Most traditional concepts of God have either removed him from the violence and destruction of the world, or else they have tried to reinterpret the negative features in order to say that we are wrong in taking these to be counter to Being and opposed to the forces of life's increase. If we now draw our insights from the vulgar, we can no longer do this. The negative can acknowledge the good and the positive, but the good and the powerful have a natural tendency to be unable to account for the evil and the powerless. Thus, to begin from the lowly and the negative actually tends less to distortion than if we begin by projecting from the top of the hierarchy of Being. Once begun, that process tends never to look back again unless it has to. Fortunately for us, the power of atheism today forces us to look back, and this concentration on the insights which our age has found in the vulgar may yet yield a more acceptable concept of God.

The flaws which lead to man's downfall must find their source in God's nature or else go unexplained. The same tendencies in man, those in which nonbeing both reveals and threatens his existence, must be present at the root of the divine nature. This possibility of imbalance and loss all too often overwhelms man; in God it may be prevented from causing destruction. In following the insights of the vulgar we uncover the source of these difficult features. Then we must move on and ask why the same structures of Being and Nonbeing, some of which are capable of so much destruction and self-destruction in man, can be contained and controlled in God? To be able to answer this is to match the insights of the vulgar with a divine insight. This is a proper democracy of Being, and the theologian is God's interpreter in his reply to the complaints of the masses.

[handwritten margin note: Sin's fall I may must go back to God]

130

CHAPTER XI

The Arguments from Denial

What could God possibly be like if he exists in spite of all the sources of argument that deny him? That is our question. In order to think about God, we need some force to shape our thought, since no specific object is given to us. Our proposal has been simple: Examine the sources which move thought toward atheism and then, moving upstream against that current, let those same forces serve as the basis for the construction of a concept of God possible for our time.

Some ideas of God seem to be incapable of withstanding much negative criticism. Any view developed in the manner we propose should, by virtue of its origin, not be so subject to this fault. We have, it is true, at each step in the argument already drawn some inferences as to what a God might be like in view of the various sources of atheism which operate constantly to deny his existence. All we intend in this present chapter is to draw these threads together explicitly. At this point we may hope to provide a clearer concept, which can serve as a basis for future systematic construction in theology.

Many views of God are possible. Among these it is the philosopher's task to try to establish criteria that can determine which might be the most likely concept, given the forces at work in a new day. One negative test is to eliminate those concepts of God which cannot stand up against the forces of atheism. Then we can move one step beyond, to ask what guidance atheism itself can give toward constructing the most likely concept

131

of God. Such procedure cannot compel belief or guarantee the existence of a Being corresponding to the concept. To the extent that it is elaborated in detail, however, the result of this process might come to have a convincing quality for anyone who considers it. There is no way to tell how successful we may be in describing God until we try—a lesson we often seem to have forgotten recently.

If thought does tend to move "away from God," we know that God is neither easily conceived nor simply approached, and this fact seems to have escaped such rationalistic philosophers as Descartes. An acute awareness of the presence of evil in the world is one of the main negative factors behind this tendency, and those who think God can be approached easily do not usually see this as such a serious problem. Thus, any concept of God must contain within itself the source of evil in a positive and not a negative sense, because the mass of men feel evil to be stronger than simply a negation of good. All those forces which tend to destroy and degrade life give us a strong impression of evil and define it for us. They appear as the sources of degeneration and deterioration present within the healthy forces of life and any fruitful exercise of its power.

The evil we find in existence did not enter of necessity. It appears to have been freely selected for our world in its amount and kind, since we see the whole order of life as contingent. Our world is fully capable of existing without its internal forces of destruction. A God who knowingly elected this mixture had sufficient power to select, from among the infinity of possible modes of Being, precisely that combination of which we find ourselves a part. Today we understand God better by his nonelections. He becomes clearer to us by what he does not do, when we compare this with other possible modes of life and how they might have been combined. We realize that God did not select for existence what remains in Nonbeing, or he included it merely in the range of potentiality present within our nature and the world as we know it.

Such a God overcomes the epistemological restrictions that have prevented his direct consideration, since he is known only as a necessary presupposition, i.e., by asking, what must God be like if atheism is possible? This approach claims neither certainty for its apprehension of God nor that God falls within simple perception. It merely asserts that what exists in fact, when considered against what might have been, can lead us to form a concept of a God needed to explain why what is in itself possible did not in fact become actual. If we follow this reasoning, we surrender certainty and necessity, but atheism has taught us that nonbelief arises precisely because it can discover no necessity in the order we have around us.

In considering atheism, we also learn to reconsider philosophy's task and its method. Those philosophical theories which restrict us from discussing God's nature lead to atheism, because any view of God which happens to be present will tend to lose its power and thus fade away in time. Philosophy, as a discussion of the most likely hypothesis, allows God to be considered by thought, although it cannot establish his nature with certitude. We must object in the name of atheism to any philosophy which restricts us to only one given view of God's nature.

The obviousness of the arguments against God indicate that he purposefully chose a concealed existence for himself in relation to the world. Such communication with him as is possible must at best be indirect. Since he is not evident, he could not have intended to offer us either an open or a direct denial of the forces which argue against his existence. Thus, any theistic view must build itself around and test itself against its ability to account for God's silence and his lack of openness. God must therefore be powerful enough to accomplish his plans without assistance. Otherwise he would be foolish to conceal himself since he should appeal directly to men for the help he needs to complete his projects.

In the face of the force of evil, we certainly seem to be dealing with a God who is capable of electing a more destructive world than necessary. Whatever good evil may accomplish, the waste around us is greater than is needed in order to achieve any simple purpose. Such a God—i.e., one who allows more chaos than is necessary and who remains never fully open to us—is a God to whom man may relate, but never in such a way that the relationship cannot fade and be lost at any moment. We discover a God

133

who allows no easy bond between himself and man, and who elected a world slightly more inclined to lead men away from him than toward him. If we face a God capable of playing a very dangerous game in his relationships to others, he must possess power sufficient for him to win in this enterprise, since it is one in which men with less power can and do lose.

Simple clarity and directness are not God's chosen means; if this is true, it must reflect something of his nature. We are faced with a God who allows both improvement and self-destruction; he is one who elected a universe which is neither impenetrable to man nor easily open to his manipulation. Construction seems to have a slight edge over deterioration, although the balance swings a little from one side to another within the established limits. The range of theory is slightly wider than the actualized forms of being, so that these can never perfectly correspond to one another, and thus theories remain forever multiple.

The difficulties in the world which lead to atheism demand that we construct our view of God in response to this question: Why is the world formed in this way rather than in another? Since we grant that worlds more advantageous to our interests are in fact possible, we must be dealing with a God who is powerful enough to fix a world's frame and to construct and select its mechanisms without being forced to one solution only. He can hold a line against our wishes. Thus, he appears to have fixed his elected universe on a course more difficult than was necessary. A God who can account for these factors will not be the easiest one to find. Were the world less violent and less conducive to atheism, it would be easier to form a concept of God, and we could have a simpler one. The path which God elected makes complexity a theoretical necessity.

We may have one God, but his nature must have a certain basic complexity, since atheism argues against a pure simplicity of principles. It also tells us that our concepts of God must be multiple, perhaps even infinite, and this is a more difficult situation for us than if only one concept of God were possible. The rejection of any given concept need not lead to atheism except in respect to that one concept. On the other hand, the problem of selecting a more adequate concept is not easy. Classical con-

134

cepts which have established themselves can serve as landmarks, but they can only go as far as to orient our selection without dictating an outcome.

Any concept of God must be such that it explains why atheism actually has slightly stronger arguments in its favor than any theism can have. A God who is merely pleasant is ruled out, and so is one who intends simply good things. The unpleasant and the destructive are his intentions too, although it is not impossible to account for them as serving some proposed ulterior motive. We are faced with a God who is capable of allowing a great deal of waste; he is apparently not interested in the most economical means. *cf Stewardship*

He must be capable of witnessing evil without being crushed by it, as we often are, since he sometimes allows it to overwhelm and to destroy us. We are led to a God who is not simply the fulfillment of our wishes, but is capable of ordering a world in which even good wishes are often blocked from being fulfilled. The God of our romantic dreams is too one-sided for any argument based upon atheism. Instead, we discover a God who combines and balances a number of forces, both good and malignant. If we meet a God who does not exempt the good man from destruction, darkness cannot be avoided in seeking such a God. If any light is to be thrown on this apparently dark side of God, it will be up to man to do so, since God has left this side of his nature in the shadows.

A God might have identified himself with one or more of the religions of the world, but whatever his associations, he seems not to have done this unreservedly or beyond question. He might have made everything unpleasant which does not directly pertain to himself, but that is not the case. Certain areas and certain practices are consecrated to God as sacred. Although he may be discovered there, he does not seem to have established an exclusive relationship with the pious. Of course, he may very well be more present in some areas than in others, and to discover where these are is the heart of our problem. That religious belief and practice can so easily be corrupted and bent to serve purely secular and selfish interests, and that secular life itself is so pleasant, and is possible to the complete exclusion of religion—

all this points to a mixture present in the divine nature itself which is at once both sacred and secular.

It is not easy to determine where God may choose to be present, and he may not always be found even where he was once discovered. Although simplicity is not absent, we are left to deal with a God who has a slight preference for complexity. Thus, he is one powerful enough to control the added divergent forces which his complexity generates. Goodness alone, then, cannot lead to God nor can simplicity or unity if taken as exclusive guides. These are at best only partial clues and reveal only partial truths about God. The religious life, however good and pure it may or may not be, is an incomplete picture too, and can even be a possibly distorting basis for constructing a theory of the divine nature.

God chose among the concepts of the world; now man must choose from among the concepts of God, except that man has been given God's original choice as one guide line which he sees before him. We can attribute "necessity" to God, but only the necessity of choosing between acceptable alternatives in order to have a world. This same necessity applies to our need to decide on a course of action, but does not extend to determine the one particular avenue which action must follow. A God capable of handling contingency is more fascinating, but also at times more horrifying. Insofar as we discuss God's intentions for the future, our arguments will lack necessity, too. We may discuss his plans, but God is not obligated to follow even a promised course. We may believe that he will, of course, but his fidelity is free, not coerced. We are dependent on his freedom for the way in which the future will unfold.

We learn something about God when we learn why concepts of him tend to die, and when we discuss in what sense he himself is capable of dying. Since concepts can die, we know that none reflects God perfectly. "Can God die?" means: Is his nature such that he may share in man's ultimate agony, death? We can answer Yes to this, if we have a concept of God capable of undergoing anguish and suffering. Men pass away in dying, but can God be affected by the forces of death and absorb destruction? Is he affected by these forces, yet still able to renew existence in the face of this process? God's life is not immune to dying, and in the world he created he removed the power to resist death ultimately, although we can postpone it. Men are capable of both major and minor renewal; we prolong or shorten life by our effort but never ultimately overcome death. Such radical power is reserved to God.

Should God himself be subject to death, we would then know him to be at best only one among a number of basic forces. If our concept of him resists death, we know that it reflects a single God who is supreme except for what he must contend with in himself. With God this internal struggle can be contained, but our own inner conflict is often destructive. The conflicts present within the world also form part of God's internal struggle, but as they are present in the world they are no longer contained forcefully enough to prevent all basic destruction. God could die in the sense of changing form radically. However, if we do not assert this, we know that he must be able to control change in order to prevent any loss of self. As men we are sometimes incapable of doing this.

When we see that concepts may die, we also learn something about our conceptual relationship to God. Certain concepts of God may be alive at times, but on the whole the natural tendency of concepts to fade does not reflect so much a death of God as it does both the multiplicity of concepts possible about a complex God and the impossibility of simple conceptualization where divinity is concerned. Not to allow the reformulation of a concept of God is to condemn it to at best a slow death. God's nature too, then, must have a certain mobility and flexibility in its balance of forces, or some one concept would be more adequate than has been the case, and would have achieved permanence as a vehicle for understanding God. This necessity for constant reformulation would be strange if God had a fixed nature. That is, if God's nature is immune to all change, as some have asserted, one concept should have managed to establish itself and to exclude all others.

As it is, this unavoidable shift in concepts reflects God's own motion. Not that he moves into and out of existence, but he does move to establish a fixed framework among the infinite variety

137

of possibles. Then he sustains this elected group, and from that point on moves only within its defined and more limited range of possibility. Such a God need not be opposed to human freedom, except that he rules out certain possibles as impossible in constructing the limits of our world. That exclusion actually promotes human freedom, since, unlike God, man can deal only with finite possibilities. As it is he fails as often as he succeeds even with this narrow range, but the actual presence of an absolute infinity of possibles would render man helpless to cope with them. God made human freedom possible by freely establishing certain limits, although these limits are themselves without internal necessity. They are only set by God's decision involving a balance of multiple value criteria.

The issue of the death of God teaches us that anyone who seeks to cling to any given concept without change may, in seeking to preserve it, actually speed its death. Metaphysics is required to revitalize any concept, since the form to be given to God takes its clue from the way Being itself is first conceptualized. God as a concept is approachable only via speculative effort, so that to omit or to deny metaphysics is to deprive us of the basis needed for thought about God. What this tells us is that, at its core, God's nature is abstract and not a single fixed quality. He is a complex of forces capable of being grasped by various formulae. Reason in man leads not to one view of God, although it may highlight several of the most likely concepts. In God, reason likewise leads him not to one conclusion but merely toward certain possible self-consistent sets. Then from among these his choice must still be made.

If we grasp all this we learn something about the limitations within which God had to work in order to combine the elements of our world into one universe. Any theory about him should reflect this self-sustaining, self-consistent quality, although more than one world and more than one concept of God can meet this criterion. In developing a view of God, metaphysical principles must be given their test for compatibility, just as in creation God is the center without which a compatible collection of possible structures could not come together to form a world. This necessary priority of "becoming" over "being" gives being a secondary position, and posits becoming as the basic category for the understanding of both Being and God.

What comes into being must suffer, and it changes in doing so. Due to this fact, God is subject to alteration, although he controls the process as men are not always able to do. Decisiveness characterizes God as well as man, although men differ from God and from each other in the degree of power they have to reach or to sustain a decision. If we speak in this way, we run the risk of making God too human, but the accumulated theological tradition acts as a needed corrective here. What we learn from tradition is that *God must be such as to be possible in the form given to him by any theory which has achieved a classical status.* Any egocentricities of an approach which is anthropologically based should next be corrected. We must account for how God could also have been correctly conceived in various classical forms, and so our contemporary understanding of man receives a needed correction from its relation to the classical concept of God.

This projects the insights we derive from human psychology onto a different plane. Particularly where freedom and contingency and decision are primary metaphysical categories, an approach to God via human nature is not an absurdity. What are simply human eccentricities can be corrected by the metaphysical tradition. From such classical study we learn how an attribute must differ in its presence in God, and this needed revision comes from the tradition and from historical concepts, not from present insight. Our insights are human, but the divine perfection, as it has been set forth in the past, eliminates from our concept what is due merely to human imperfection.

The forces of atheism teach us to construct a view of God which will be capable of providing clear and distinct answers. Our need is for a God with whom one may argue directly. Those forces which lead men to atheism can only be resisted by a God who is capable of replying to the charges brought against him, although it is man who speaks for God through the view of the divine which he constructs. A few individuals may be persuaded to forget what first forced them toward atheism by moving to take refuge in a mystical doctrine. However, this is not an "an-

139

swer" to atheism, nor does it lead to a God constructed in line with those forces, as we have suggested here.

If Being and thought cannot be identical, the relation of our concepts to God cannot be a fixed one. Some concepts obviously do express God's nature and can thus serve as vehicles for his apprehension, but their ability to do this is not self-guaranteed, and it may be lost. Concepts tend to shift; they do not seem to "move at the same speed" that God does. Thus, human effort is required in order to mold and reshape any concept so that it will still be theologically useful. What this tells us about God is that he is evidently neither completely detached from verbal forms nor completely expressible within them. God's relations to thought, and through thought to words, is necessarily indirect. It never involves identity, except perhaps at passing moments of contact and insight. Nor is God such as to initiate overt action to prevent both this constant loss of power in any concept of him and the consequent drift toward atheism. All action that is intended to revive any concept of God must come from man. If his effort fails, the words and thoughts which have been traditionally used to lead to God will move us away from God quite naturally. They no longer describe him or achieve much solidity as a basis for thought.

God must be such in nature as to be apprehended and expressed in a variety of ways, and his being must possess more than one side. Atheism sometimes develops because any side of God once apprehended, e.g., love, is taken too simply as defining God's whole nature, and then this characteristic may come into conflict with another side, e.g., the power to be destructive. The various aspects of God must all exist in him so as not to be assimilated one to another; instead they are held together in a flexible federation. To oversimplify this situation in favor of any one attribute, such as compassion, is to invite atheism when that attractive simplicity proves too superficial.

That the attributes of God are capable of shifting in their relationship to one another does not necessarily indicate an imperfection in God, that is, if he is in perfect control of all these possible relationships. However, this does help to explain why atheism has a certain naturalness, since neither the world nor

God seems to be organized so as always to lead inevitably toward a single center. Our directional orientation is not so simple, and this is the source of some confusion. Out of this situation atheism can arise, since there is a source in God's very nature for the mind's deflection in its attempt to think about him. His complex nature rejects simple thought.

This again points to the difficulty which any thought, and even more any verbal expression, will encounter in attempting to grasp God adequately, and why its success can only be momentary and is in need of constant renewal. This situation also points to the fact that God's nature is not subject to simple fixity. If it were, it would not explain the lack of a fixed form for its expression. The mind can grasp and express more easily what does not change; Plato is right on this point. Thus, our conceptual difficulty with God indicates his lack of eternal fixity. Atheism is too strong if God is not difficult to grasp conceptually. Sometimes this has been thought to be because he transcends Being. Our suggestion is that one of the reasons is that his nature has a degree of flexibility in its very constitution. The fault lies as much with God's nature as with the inadequacies of our conceptualization.

Even on a univocal theory of Being, the first question remains: How does the application of, say, change differ between man and God? *Control* is perhaps the central issue here, since men destroy themselves by uncontrolled change. This aspect of change need not apply to God, and the deterioration which comes when man overreaches himself and attempts something beyond his power is also unknown within the divine nature. Aristotle thought change indicated a deficiency in any nature subject to it, and thus he and countless later theologians were unwilling to attribute change to God. In some sense, of course, change must represent deficiency, but what we question is whether it must always be a complete imperfection. If God always remains capable of achieving any goal, even if an intervening freedom puts off its accomplishment to a future time, to seek a goal is not an imperfection if there is no lack of power present to achieve that end eventually. God may even surrender his ability to determine an outcome in certain areas, e.g., human action. However, if this

141

prerogative is freely surrendered, it is a gift and not a loss in divine terms.

God must himself be very metaphysical, and by this I mean that his nature must combine at its core all of the central metaphysical attributes, e.g., unity, infinity, time, etc. Since we have just released God from human bondage and allowed him to change, he is always the first metaphysician. That is, he operates with the various possible combinations of first principles after having elected one collection to form the confederation which now loosely structures our world. We may consider other possible combinations which might have governed our world, but God constantly engages in such metaphysical calculation. Holding firm to the principles which he elected for creation, he may still rearrange these principles in various combinations in his thought. In this sense his mind always moves, since, as against what is actual, the possibles are infinitely larger, and nothing necessitates the particular details of our combination as it was selected. Since God's mind can move, he eludes our grasp if our thought tries to fix him at one point, and this makes our fixed formulae go out of date if not constantly revived and revised.

Yet, since possible concepts of God are many, and since to reach atheism regarding any one idea of God is often to begin to consider others, this tendency from atheism back to theism yields certain clues in itself. For instance, God cannot be completely detached from our world. One concept of him is related to others, and our mind, in moving among these, in some way moves on the fringes of the divine nature too. That is, God himself could be in more than one form, e.g., those which various philosophers have used to conceive him. Being God, he combines them all, although not exactly in the way specified by each concept. The elements of God may be formed and put together into concepts by other metaphysicians in various ways so that, in apprehension, he appears to assume different forms.

He is perhaps the God whom the atheist rejects, but he is this in the mode of not-being. This is why a rejected concept can in turn lead back to theism, since God in some sense is that atheistic concept, but just not precisely in the way the atheist thinks of him. The concepts of God which he is not—those he might

142

be. He is these by negation, or he may be grasped by them partially if proper portions are extracted. No adequate view of God can be uncomplex, so that any one may be partly right and partly wrong. God's nature actually reflects every attribute that can be applied, but sometimes in the mode of nonbeing and sometimes in a different degree of being than proposed by one particular concept.

"Emotion" has often been thought of as a deficiency, but now it can become a virtue and may be applied to God as well as to man. Men experience emotion, but sometimes they are blinded by it rather than moved to deeper penetration. Emotion is present in God; it is felt and yet controlled. It is able to direct and to inspire action, and yet it never breaks Being apart in the way it can be disruptive in a man who is less equipped to control it. "To suffer" is not always to be degraded; it may mean to be purified. Only when men block and resist it does suffering have a totally debasing effect. No single set of attributes locks God's nature in. All attributes equally apply, although all insight depends on seeing just how these are arranged in relation to one another in the various possible concepts of God.

The fixity of one concept of God would depend upon the dominance of one attribute in his nature. If the vulgar have taught us a rough democracy among the divine attributes (although even in a democracy there must be leadership), we understand why concepts will shift and fade and also why atheism always tends to set in. That God may be discerned among the vulgar indicates the possibility of always passing back from atheism to theism, since he may be reached from literally any starting point.

Since the constant threat of Nonbeing is almost more crucial to man than are the modes of Being, Nonbeing must also be applicable to God if he is to explain this important fact. Here again suffering has a basis upon which it can be attributed to God too. This teaches us something about God's power, for we know him not to fail in undergoing suffering. Our failures come when we cannot sustain ourselves under the pressure of suffering, so that *the primary difference between man and God emerges in the absolute sufficiency of power in God.* For men this quantity is limited and causes us constantly to struggle for control as we suffer. It is in experiencing God's suffering that we learn of the extent of his power.

God purifies both himself and us by his ability to be present in the lowest, since to find God in the unexpected depths of Being's horrors is a much more realistic experience than to find him in a peaceful silence and solitude. He may, of course, be found in quiet contemplation, but the beautiful heights can no longer be the most undistorted place from which to derive our concepts of God. Flaws are not absent from his nature, but they are not infectious; he can hold imperfections back from producing internal destruction. Once disharmony enters our life, on the other hand, it may undermine every established form.

God could not make us equal to him in power, a fact which Plato reported in the *Timaeus*, and thus he opened us to destruction from within as well as without. "Power," then, is the key divine attribute; and in the face of this discovery men have traditionally humbled themselves in respect. However, we no longer act like the peasants of old who felt God's nature to be above their own in purity. Today we are humbled in discovering God's nature as identical to ours at the core of Being in spite of his vast superiority of power. He is able to contain the disruption of Nonbeing through his superior power, while we mortals are prone to experience failure more often than success.

This Chap. summary & his conclusions about God —

CHAPTER XII

God, Freedom, and the Devil

> "The Devil is alive and well
> and living in hell."

One of atheism's strongest incentives in modern times has been the desire to free man from God's dominance. What can we say now about this central concern? Must God be denied for man to be free? If we had to select one cause for the rise in atheism in the modern world in addition to the problem of evil, man's search for freedom probably would be the most likely candidate. For several centuries the struggle to free all men has been going on. The early Christian gospel announced spiritual freedom but accepted political slavery; today that will not do. In some areas this contemporary quest has succeeded with considerable success, but even when it has not been achieved, it is still the dominant modern dream.

Man now feels that he possesses the means to find liberty and to rise to equality with his rulers. It does not seem to matter whether or not this power is poorly used. Men will have freedom today if they can, even at the price of disrupting a "higher culture" and at the risk of chaos. In the majority of theological traditions, God has been identified with necessity, with foreknowledge, and with a fixity of the future. Thus, in achieving human freedom, it has often seemed that it is God who must first be opposed.

Let us begin to consider freedom by giving a technical statement for the kind of God which the powerful forces of atheism have led us to as the only God capable of survival today. God is always conceived of in terms of certain key concepts, and these vary in their definition. First we will set out what seem to be God's characteristics as they have emerged in the course of this argument, and then the issue of freedom can be considered in that context. We have argued that whenever God is discussed one must always ask, "Which God?" It follows that human freedom and atheism can only be considered in the light of some one particular concept of God and not all of them at once. We can test the "God of evil" we have built up in the course of this argument by first outlining that deity in technical detail. After that, we can return to press the issue of freedom against this God as a test of his strength.

(1) *Nonbeing.* Since atheism asserts the nonexistence of God, any view which builds upon its insights will have to give primacy to Nonbeing. Negation, and all negative argument, rests upon the awareness of a lack of power and of an inability to fulfill existence in some way. Asking the question of God's existence more than any other question makes us conscious of the continual possibility of nonbeing, and a threat to existence comes with the constant possibility of a negative reply to our inquiries. In questioning God's existence we first meet Nonbeing unavoidably, and we must deal with it there at the outset.

Nonbeing illuminates the meaning of Being, because it stands for the absolutely infinite modes of Being, most of which must of necessity remain nonexistent. Having arisen from this, every being is constantly surrounded by it, and to slip back into the Nonbeing that surrounds us is a constant possibility. Man is his nonbeing; he is his future, which he is not yet and may never become. He is both his past, which no longer exists in its full power, and the sea of things he may become, which surrounds him and in which his nature "swims about" constantly. What man is not (past, future, potentials, impossibilities) is always greater than what he is, so that "being" comes to mean this: an ability to sustain the power to exist and to act rather than to be

146

overwhelmed and immobilized by the ever-present threat of lapsing into Nonbeing.

The full range of Nonbeing includes all unfulfilled potentials. Some perhaps will never exist in fact, and these are the possibles which were rendered impossible (except for thought) in God's original choice of the world's frame. The range of Nonbeing forms the material of God's nature. It surrounds us, and constitutes the limits within which God works in creation. Fortunately, we are only aware of a small portion of its extent at any one time, or we would drown in its vastness. In theory, our mind can take in the whole range of Nonbeing, but it can only do this sequentially, abstractly, and a little at a time. It grasps Being too, but that scope is less wide. What is, is always more limited than what is not; thus thought is wider than Being alone. In its concrete detail, the mind takes in and can deal with only one area at a time. God constantly attends to all Nonbeing in its full range, although he does not give equal attention to all areas. This depends on what decisions he has made or intends to make.

God takes in the full range of Being and Nonbeing, but his attention never "slips"; he can simultaneously apprehend every mode and detail. His power is commensurate with its full range; even in limited instances ours sometimes is not. Thus, God constantly controls Nonbeing and the passage into and out of actual existence. We do when we are successful, but we often fall victim to nonbeing, i.e., we lose ourselves in its vastness and waste our limited power. God set a limit to Being's power, and then set it adrift in a sea of Nonbeing. Here is where our decisions are to be made; God was voluntarily assumed and limited himself to the role of observer.

(2.) *Being.* We come to understand the meaning of Being through Nonbeing. This is because, insofar as we focus only on what is, we cannot understand the magnitude of our problem or the dependence of our particular mode of being on nonbeing. That is, to face the threat of loss and the possibilities for new forms of being, we must be aware of what we are in relation to all that is not. "To be" means to possess a power sufficient to sustain a concrete mode of being against its passage into Nonbeing. Furthermore, and more important for our creative and progressive ability, to be means to be able to grasp a mode of Nonbeing which is such that it might come to be. This happens when the power to bring it to existence is offered to it either by us, by nature, or by God.

Sometimes it is not possible for a particular mode of nonbeing to which we hold to achieve existence. This is true at least at a particular time, but it may never be possible within our world as it is constituted now. If so, then power is wasted; it falls and dissipates itself in nonbeing. We can accept our existence uncritically, but, whether intuitively or consciously and verbally, we know what we are and what we can and cannot become only to the extent that we are able to fathom the range of Nonbeing. What we need to see mirrored in Nonbeing is both Being itself in general and our mode of being in particular.

In God the modes of Nonbeing are numerically far greater than the modes of Being, but God is not the victim of this threat, since he has given existence or actual being to a portion of that which is possible. Taken individually, he could have given the power to exist to any particular mode of Nonbeing, but given the conditions for a universe, not all of these are mutually compatible. The selection of some modes (e.g., ours) forever excludes the existence of all modes which are incompatible with the basic conditions for our world once they were determined. "To be" for God means to maintain constant control over the range of Nonbeing and the conditions under which it may or may not receive existence, except for those areas of control now delegated to man.

Nonbeing is not "outside" God's nature; it forms his body, so to speak. His being is his control of this, although nothing prevents him from relinquishing direct control over any given portion. Inside our world he allows man the freedom to deal with Nonbeing under the particular set of laws given to it. "To be" for God means never to be forced to act by the threat of Nonbeing, except to create at least something against the threat of total Nonbeing. Except in the areas which he has set free from his control, his power makes him immune to forced action under

148

i. How can any religious identify man with God as neo psychology.

duress. Man achieves that state only rarely and with great effort. His control is always precarious and subject to his ability to maintain a delicate balance. This situation clearly distinguishes man from God.

Yes - tho wp are most relaxed when we're in that position.

3. *Power.* The link between Being and Nonbeing is power, and without this Being could neither sustain itself nor Nonbeing come to be. Power can also take negative forms, since Nonbeing has the power to threaten existence. This comes about not by positive action but through the attraction exerted by a negative force. Thus, power in itself is neither good nor bad. By its agency all that is good comes to be, but so does all that is destructive. Power is the ability to actualize or sustain a mode of existence, but it may also mean to enhance or to improve that mode, or to bring from nonbeing some other mode to be grafted into Being's frame.

Resurrection is power.

Of itself power has no rational form; it takes its structure only from what it empowers to be. When it destroys, it does this by breaking out of one mold and pouring into another, or else propels one mode of being to interfere with another in a way that injures or destroys. Since power is limited by the structure that dictates what is possible and what is impossible, it either wastes itself or destroys others if it is directed to give being to what is impossible. This involves both what is not possible in itself (i.e., self-contradictory) and what is not compossible either at that time or absolutely.

Men vary by nature in their possession of power and in its type. Some have a greater ability for rational apprehension, and this means that their minds are propelled through the entire range of the absolute infinity of possibles in their thought. Others have greater creative power, and this means an ability to give existence to new modes of being through a control over Nonbeing. Since men's thoughts exceed the range of what is actual, just as Nonbeing exceeds Being, human power is always directed toward what is not except when it turns to destroy what is. Since what can come into existence is limited, and men's power and vision always exceed it, human power continually tends to turn inward and to become involved in mutual struggle. In this situation of conflict, particular beings are often crushed or lost. In

149

order to sustain his existence God does not compete, as men do with each other and with nature, in this conflict to establish and sustain power over other forms of existence. This is perhaps the fundamental difference between God and man.

Our power could not be infinite in its range. It had to be given some definite extent, but it did not have to have the particular range it now has. Were its scope greater, our creative ability would be increased, but so would our ability to wield power destructively. Our power might have been restricted against causing destruction, but God seems to have set for us a more dangerous and violent path than such a restrained world would allow. In this way our life is more akin to the divine in that it shares more extensively in the range of Nonbeing known to God than it might have if God had chosen a safer path for us. Unfortunately, our power is not always equal to dealing with such vast extremes. In the narrow passageway God has assigned to being, our power can turn upon itself and destroy, and it often does this in reacting against the threat of the vastness of Nonbeing which we feel unable to control. It is, unfortunately, easier to destroy than to create, although both avenues are open to us in proportion to our circumstances.

4. *Evil.* In the face of the power of atheism, our method has been to gather the forces of evil into one center. This we have personified as the Devil in contrast to God, although our aim was to construct a concept of God. To do this we allowed ourselves to be guided by the necessity to include these negative forces in our account. The only possible answer to atheism is to take all the forces that drive toward it and see if there is a God who could accept these into his own nature. In its starkest form, evil means the destruction of what has a right to exist, but in its milder form it involves a draining or a crippling of the power of existence. Some of this comes about through natural forces. However, God must bear the responsibility for unleashing those wild powers upon us indiscriminately. He alone can account for setting the limits on our power and knowledge just exactly where they are. The odds assigned to us in this struggle are not impossible, but they are certainly not the most favorable either.

All existence is not destroyed under the impact of evil forces.

150

Renewing life is often possible, and men may protect themselves and even lessen destruction when it comes. However, the level of the natural violence which we face has been fixed by God in spite of the fact that nature might have been more pastoral and all-friendly in the setting it provides for us. Human destruction and the evil involved in the loss of existence or in its disfiguring when it need not be—for all this men are directly responsible. However, it is God who fixed the mode of our existence which allows this to be possible when it need not have been exactly as it is.

Within himself God is not evil, because his power is such as to sustain his existence without loss or threat. Only in the particular created order which he selected and within which we live does God's own potential for evil become actual. This is because the power given to us ordinarily is sufficient to sustain existence, but our limited energy is also such that it is able to destroy and to interfere with others. Our power was not fixed rigidly as to its patterns, although generally it flows through our existing modes of Being. It does this except when it breaks out of control, and then it can produce insanity or physical damage or simply unhappiness.

We are free not to be, and this is true in the face of the fact that our power might have been fixed in one mode of existence and not allowed to depart from it voluntarily. The full extent of Nonbeing is open to us, and this makes us closer to God in the range our being can cover, at least in thought if not in fact. Since our power is less than his, our efforts are partially blind. They compete with other beings and destroy whenever we lose control. We could have been made to exist as just an intellectual observer to the infinite range of Nonbeing, but God elected to let a portion of its fury sweep over us. This usually purifies and invigorates us, but insofar as it destroys, the vastness of the range of Nonbeing open to us is also the source of evil. This was fixed in its amount by God's election, and, in spite of our protests, we have no choice but to deal with the situation given to us as best we can.

3. *Good.* Like Being, good is to be defined by a prior grasp of evil and by what makes such destruction possible. What is good

151

is not simply what exists; it must include what has power to sustain itself against Nonbeing and to resist the threat of evil's destruction. However, this holding action is only the beginning of goodness. In the face of what challenges it, to be good is not simply to resist but to be able to rise against corrosive forces. "Being good" means to enhance what exists and to bring new possible modes from Nonbeing into existence as part of Being. Thus, goodness also means selective discrimination, i.e., to support in existence what will enhance it rather than simply clash and destroy. This might be a simple matter if our value norms were not multiple and sometimes themselves in conflict.

Potentially destructive forces are often contained within what is beautiful, so that good involves not merely an absence of evil but the containing of those creative powers within some form of being. Some good forms cannot be given life within our present actual structure. That which is good is that which draws from any mode of being its maximum controlled power for existence, whether this is in the training of a football player, the creative capacity of an artist, or the simplicity of daily existence.

God is good because he continually controls evil within his own nature. He is not good to the extent that he allows unnecessary destruction to rain down on human existence, although it must be remembered that this is as much a part of his nature as are the forces that produce good. In this sense we can realize in our life what it is impossible for God to do, since in him negative forces are held in check and cannot break loose to destroy. It is not a good thing that men are able to actualize terrors which God cannot, but if we see that men have this ability, it is true and revelatory of Being's relation to Nonbeing and to power. Men have the capacity to control power and to direct it away from destruction, but this is a contingent affair for men, due to the limits set on the range of their power and knowledge. Our freedom lies in the control or in the loss of control of such power as we have. We balance it between evil and good, between various kinds of good, and between Nonbeing and Being.

(6) *Will.* Obviously will is the central concept for a theory of the divine nature which is based on an argument from the exis-

tence of the Devil. Were the negative forces we have personified in the Devil not existent, a theory of Being could be constructed which did not give primacy to "will" as an interpretive category. However, now we can see why this should be done and why will is a primary principle. What is important to remember is that the powers of evil which do exist and threaten us do not exist of necessity. Had God shut them out, he might have contained them in himself and thus spared us. Such was not his decision, evidently, and a line which defines the limits of power can be drawn and held to only through the decisiveness of will. Will, of course, simply means the execution of power, but it is not identical with power. In itself power exists simply as energy which can be expended; this is limited in supply for us but infinite for God. Will is what triggers this release, and in that sense it is as important as power, since without the action of will, power would not of necessity assume any form or direction.

Clearly in its assigned relation to power will is itself a kind of power. This is true in the sense that nonbeing is not and yet in a sense is, and is related to actual being. Will depends upon an association with knowledge, and this means a grasp of the forms or modes of Being and Nonbeing. Knowledge in itself is not power (let alone virtue). Will is that crucial and necessary and slender intermediary which either releases power under the control of knowledge or else moves against it for destruction. Chaos, if given the power to break forth, always destroys, but knowledge can also be destructive. This indicates the priority of evil over good and the lack of any necessity inhering in what is good. That is, before any good can come to be or be sustained, evil must be understood or else we may fail to contain its destructive power.

All things great—great goods and great evils alike—owe their existence or nonexistence to the crucial direction of will. It in turn is based on a relation between knowledge and power, between Being and Nonbeing, between good and evil, and yet it is not identical with any of these. "Understanding" means the grasp of a plurality of interdependent factors. No one of these exists alone, but when taken together they define the possible limits of existence.

7) Possibility. Basic to and underlying every structure is the absolutely infinite range of the possible modes of Being and Nonbeing, since from this all being is brought into existence. The totality of these modes in some sense are and define God. Since they are not limited by sequential time, all possible modes of Being have been and are held in God. The possible kinds of being are infinite, and within each attribute (as Spinoza called them) an infinity of varieties is possible. Corresponding to each, perhaps reflected as its shadow, is a parallel mode of nonbeing. Each may exist and each may not exist. This depends on the laws regulating existence, the exercise of power, the direction of will, and the rules established to govern these transitions.

There is always less in existence than is held in nonexistence, since the selection of certain laws (e.g., noncontradiction, gravity, a boiling point for water) automatically excludes from existence more than they make possible under their imposed conditions. As the possibles which underly all actual existence are grasped, Being and Nonbeing as specific structures are brought forth from that realm which is itself without limits. God is understood as the master of this realm, without which no specific structure could have come into existence at all in the face of all that is possible. We need to discover the limits of Being and Nonbeing, but in order to do this we must go behind them to the absolutely infinite range of possibles from which God brought forth both and defined them.

Possibility also defines the Devil. Since no form of existence is necessary, malignant forces are no less possible than constructive forces, and our world includes its share of both. These proportions need not have been fixed in the exact combination in which we find them, but we understand the context of creation when we grasp the full range of all that was originally possible, and when we understand how the moment of creation ruled out all but a narrow range as it established certain laws to govern existence. We grasp possibility in general, and we do this primarily within the limits of our own actualized structure. Possibility is every mode of Being and Nonbeing of which God's absolutely infinite intellect can conceive. It includes even those whose conception or existence would involve a contradiction.

Depending on the skill of our grasp, we operate with a wider or narrower range of these possibles, but God attends immediately to every possible. He does this first in detachment from their incorporation in any particular structure, and secondarily, he views the possibles through the special conditions which he has imposed upon them (e.g., natural laws). To dissolve back down every actual existent to its original place among the possibles, or to work forward from the possibles to some new form of existence—this is to see the world at least partially from God's perspective. For him possibility precedes actually. In our life this is not the case; in our knowledge possibility becomes our goal and the source of our enlightenment regarding actualities, but first we have to work our way back from the actualities we now immediately perceive.

8. *Infinity*. Whatever we perceive is always some finite quantity or quality, whether given its limits out of the infinity of the possibles by God or by man. That which is possible in itself tends toward infinity and cannot impose limits on itself, i.e., it cannot achieve for itself those conditions which are necessary if it is to come to be in fact. Power, will, and knowledge—all three must combine to do this. What this indicates is that our mind (vs. our eyes) by its nature tends more toward infinity, and thus our mind is more able to cope with such an expanse. The mind's function is to impose limits in order to hold knowledge, but it can grasp infinity without difficulty, or at least this is true at the height of man's full power.

What is involved in infinity varies in its inherent tendency toward a lack of limits. It resists restrictive limits in various degrees, and in the range and kind of possibles, tends toward a complete lack of limit. Once we were fearful of the mind's inability to cope with a lack of limit, and Aristotle's metaphysics illustrates this fear of the inhibiting effects of unlimitedness. Now we see that, for all its danger, limitlessness is needed if we are to have a basic grasp of our world's structure. Moreover, we have developed better techniques (mathematical and mechanical) for dealing with this difficulty, and a tendency toward infinity has the advantage of freeing the mind from its particular present restrictions. This is a crucial experience which we need to live through, since we now find no necessity in the limits we most immediately encounter, either in our natural world, in our constructed existence, or in our knowledge of both.

9. *Knowledge.* By its relation to infinity, i.e., to the complete range of the possible modes of Being and Nonbeing, knowledge is defined. Various combinations of modes are possible within our defined framework, and to grasp what these are and the conditions upon which their existence depends—this is to possess knowledge. To go further and go beyond the laws that define what is potential within our life, to grasp the relation of our order to other possible orders, this is man's knowledge as it approaches God's. Such comprehension is not at all an idle luxury, for many minds grasp a mode of Being which would be perfectly possible in some other world, but is just not possible to actualize in our own. In order to know what can possibly be, we have to learn structures beyond the limits of our own particular form of being. The actual alone does not tell us what is possible.

As long as these modes remain in concept only (as in science fiction), they can be entertaining and even enlightening. However, when someone does not understand our world's relation to orders now excluded from existence, he can rain havoc on himself and on others. He may try to give existence to a possible mode whose actual existence was excluded from our world at creation, (e.g., an element excluded in establishing the periodic table), or at least one which is prohibited from existing in the particular time and place now suggested for it. Destruction results when we have not exerted ourselves to go outside our world in order to grasp the relation of the possible to the impossible, because then we do not control our power accordingly, and thus not effectively.

10. *Transcendence.* God does transcend actual Being, but then so does Nonbeing. He also transcends both, in the sense that he possesses the power, the will, and the knowledge to reach a decision regarding the actualization of some set or sets from among the possibles. All of these attributes men also possess, since men follow this divine process in knowledge, although they do so with varying degrees of power and success. In that sense God transcends neither man nor the world. Of course, in the sense that our world forms only a small selection of the possibles,

God transcends the world. Men are not limited to the actual world for their valid thought, in spite of the attempts of some philosophers to restrict them only to what is empirically given. In that sense God transcends man less than he does the world. The existence which God selected for the world, however, was such as to be independent, i.e., to have its own power to exist outside of his nature.

Still, in the ways already outlined, God does operate differently, and thus he acts in ways in which man cannot. Although no different faculties are involved, God transcends man in the way in which he exercises them. This difference, although one of degree, is absolutely crucial in defining and understanding both man and God and their relationship. In the strict sense, God does not transcend knowledge, since knowledge means to grasp the modes of Being and Nonbeing and their possible combinations. This men can do as well as God, although men never grasp all modes simultaneously as God can and must. This defines the way in which God transcends human knowledge and also the way in which men never grasp him just as he is.

II. *Personality.* If the world's structure were necessary, we might restrict the characteristics of personality only to man. Since the range of possibility is wider than the conditions for actuality (e.g., the law of noncontradiction), the power to actualize requires the presence of the attributes of personality (i.e., will, power, and knowledge in effective combination). God must embody these central structures of personality too, or he would never have reached a decision regarding the particular form our world was to take. The fact that we have a world is our evidence that a decision was arrived at and that it is the result of the essential characteristics of personality in the divine nature. Certain shaping mechanisms are built into this process, but the selection of these mechanisms as against others that are possible requires a decisive power inherent only in traits of personality.

We do not argue from the nature of man to the attribution of personality to God. Instead, it is an understanding of the contingency of our world's form that requires the essentials of personality in a concept of God in order to explain how it was possible for anything at all to come to be. After this, the same qualities

157

of personality can then be discerned more clearly in man, only now they operate in a restricted form. Understanding how God must operate provides our model for man. All statements about man must be translated into statements about God in order to be understood properly.

12.) *Unity.* To personify the forces of evil in the Devil, or the powers of goodness in God, is not a falsification but a necessity, that is if we accept the crucial role of personality in all selection for existence or destruction. The larger problem where God is concerned, however, is the unity of all his attributes. According to some classical theories, unity is the first attribute of divinity, and it does have a valuable ability to guide and control the role assigned to the other attributes of God and to determine the forms of Being and Nonbeing brought into existence. Nevertheless, as we have noted elsewhere,* unity tends to exclude both personality and a plurality of ultimate attributes in God and then to lead to a transcendence of all knowledge.

Why have we chosen another route in constructing this present view of God when so much classical theology has accepted the primacy of unity? The present procedure considers unity last rather than first, and this obviously leads to different results where our concept of God is concerned. Our proposal was to examine the forces leading to atheism, to personify the powers of evil, and then construct a view of God from the insight to be found here. Unity, when it is allowed a priority among the divine attributes, tends to favor goodness as its second expression (cf. Plotinus and his use of "Good" as a second name for the "One"). When unity dominates, it cannot assign much power to the negative and the destructive, since they always work against unity.

"Giving the Devil his due" is what prevents us from seeing unity (or goodness) as the primary divine attribute. A plurality of attributes held together in personality—this now becomes a maximum allowable unity if God's existence is based on an argument from denial. We are faced with a God whose attributes are joined more flexibly than in most classical concepts. In this

---

*See my *Divine Perfection: Possible Ideas of God* (New York: Harper & Row, 1961).

case, the theologian's first problem is to give an adequate account of how God prevents internal destruction. If given a similarly loose structure, man often is not able to sustain self-preservation. On this less strict application of unity, evil is assigned a much more fundamental role in the divine nature. Nevertheless, the self-sufficiency of God and the limited independence of man—these account for both evil's containment in God and also for its outbursts in man.

In the sketch of the divine (and human) attributes given above, freedom was not listed as one of the selected twelve. Why not, when admittedly this is at the very center of the modern concern, and its demands are a major force leading toward atheism? Our answer is: because freedom is not an attribute in itself. *It is the description of how all the structures function together, and this is somewhat different for man than for God.* Unity excludes a looseness of structure, but that is the primary condition which freedom requires. Thus, *considering how to achieve unity last rather than first is perhaps precisely what provides us with the conditions for human freedom.* Freedom depends upon contingency, i.e., that nothing ultimately need be as it is except that certain decisions have made it so, whether this comes from God originally or from man secondarily. This situation requires a flexibility among the various aspects of Being and Nonbeing. Also, a similar flexibility must exist among the forces that govern Being-itself, i.e., will, power, and knowledge as exercised in different ways by both God and man.

Time has not been treated as a primary attribute either, although neither has eternity been given any special priority. Time must also be taken as a derivative aspect within Being. God in his nature is capable of motion, although this neither takes a physical form, as it does with us, nor tends to destruction beyond his control. Since God has not come into existence (excluding for the moment the Christmas story), time in the sense of beginning does not apply to him. In moving to give the world its frame from among all possible worlds, God gives our form of time its beginning. In that sense he is himself in time in his creative action and is related to it. Since God's nature is flexible in its relation of parts and is not immune to all motion, no difficulty

159

arises simply from such an application of time to God. All that is required is that the particular sense of the attribution must be stated specifically so that we do not thoughtlessly include in our description of God the limiting aspects of our particular mode of sharing in time.

Although there are many roads that lead to atheism, it has been the theme emerging in this essay that two seem to be central in the modern era and to have the most to do with atheism's present strength. These are (1) the force of evil or the problem of theodicy, and (2) the question of man's freedom. Beginning as we have with the symbol of the Devil, the question of whether God can justify his ways to man has tended to become more important, although perhaps in a more silent way it is man's intense desire to be free that most often causes him to get rid of God.

The question of man's freedom may now be answered briefly. To do this is not to launch a different enterprise; it is simply one way of bringing into sharper focus the concept of God which has been emerging in opposition to atheism. Freedom is not a simple question, but the construction of an ethical theory is a kind of first fruits of any new philosophical insight. Yet ethics is oriented by its metaphysics, so that we can test the concept of God which has been emerging by applying it to the question of freedom. The result of doing this is not simply ethics, but rather a metaphysical starting point and a chance to concentrate the concept of God on one crucial point. The issue is whether God's existence must be denied for man to be free. Many if not all theological and metaphysical views claim that they champion "freedom." That all men claim it while not agreeing about its nature merely indicates that the meaning of freedom is derivative, and that it changes according to the metaphysical context.

Since God has most recently been rejected in the name of freedom, the relation of God to freedom has again become a pressing problem. What we must do now is to test the view of God which has been emerging in this essay by applying it to the question of freedom. Let us begin by asking the crucial question: In what sense is God free as he moves to create the world? Then, next, we can compare this to man's freedom, and both may be considered in the context of the twelve concepts outlined just above.

Freedom never means to act without any restriction, and this fact is consistent with our having called freedom a derived concept and not a basic attribute. Since it is conditioned by an understanding of how God's attributes come together, freedom is one result of how that analysis is concluded. The issue is whether any flexibility is possible among the attributes themselves or whether they operate together necessarily and in fixed relationships. In order to determine this we cannot start with freedom. We must set out the first principles of a metaphysics, and only then can we see what freedom is.

Given the power and extent of Nonbeing, God has no choice but to create. In that sense God is also coerced by Nonbeing. The nonbeing which is internal to his nature is so vast that God's nature would remain too unspecific unless he gave existence to some portion of it. That is, he causes Nonbeing to pass over into Being. Goodness tends to communicate itself and so does power; both are self-diffusive. They move God to create by working to develop cohesive sets from all the possibles which are constantly present in Nonbeing. His nature is generous and not grudging, just as Platonists have always declared.

Evil in a sense forces his action too, since if nothing were created its power would remain unopposed. Positive beings must be constituted before there can be any centers for either resistance or further creation, although God could simply "hold the fort alone" if he chose to. To create is to establish something concrete in the face of evil. God can contain all these forces within himself, but their combination in his nature is such as to cause him to tend toward creation as an outlet. Nonbeing is not in itself evil, but if God gave nothing existence for fear of the resulting destruction, this would be to give evil dominance by default within the nonbeing of all possibles, since goodness demands existence in order to be effective.

God could withhold this and refrain from all creation; his power is sufficient to hold out against us all. Yet he would have to do this by moving against his own nature. This is not impossible, but clearly it is not preferable, and God is not forced to take a second best alternative as men so often must. What is open to God in freedom is, so to speak, the choice of the time and the place and the conditions. The nature of all possible entities in themselves make some combinations impossible, if compossibility and noncontradiction are accepted as criteria. Beyond that, more is possible than can be created. To have this available surplus of alternatives is the very meaning of freedom for both God and men. Since God's alternatives are greater, his freedom is wider, but so is his ability to control Nonbeing and destruction.

The possibles taken in themselves reach to absolute infinity. If he did not impose the law of noncontradiction, God might have brought all of this absolute infinity of entities and states into existence simultaneously, although chaos would rule such a creation. Time, space, number, and even beauty, all could have been based on different systems. A two-valued logic governs our world in fact, but not of necessity. Thus, even under the conditions needed for consistent life, God is able to choose from among a wide variety of possible systems, each of which has its own advantages and disadvantages. No one is superior in all respects, and this fact makes the contingent action of will so important. *Miracles come – because no ideal world* is

In such a situation as this, will is the only power which can render decision possible after reason has calculated the advantages and disadvantages of each alternative open to the flow of power. We have double evidence that a personal will did choose the conditions assigned to this life. That is, we know that our particular scheme is not the most perfect order possible. All possible value criteria can never be forced into one hierarchy. This less-than-optimum situation can only be dealt with by a deliberate act of will, i.e., one which draws the line somewhere below the calculated optimum and is capable of holding it there.

When the conditions themselves cannot dictate a single outcome, creation comes about only through the mediation of a will which is powerful enough to enforce and sustain its decision. Time has a form of existence in the divine nature; however, God's options are the creation of place, its conditions, and also the explicit form which time will take. Even if place were not created, time would have its function in God. Moving constantly against Nonbeing and in opposition to the disruptive forces, which once they are loose in the world will be termed evil, God chooses his own specific conditions for the passage from indefinite Nonbeing into some particular form of being.

God established those intricate systems which scientists will later uncover, including the particular conditions and procedures for evolutionary creation and natural selection. In doing this he gave his creation an artificial form of the unity which he himself has by nature. This is not a dominating unity but a flexible conjunction of various attributes. Ironically enough for those who have attributed unity to God as a primary attribute, only a created order could be embraced by that kind of rigidity. God himself is above the dominance of unity, and fortunately he compromised its possible rigidity in creating our particular order. He did not allow unity to dominate, so that *our freedom comes about because we are allowed to share in the precarious balance of attributes which define God, although unfortunately this must be without his power of full control.*

In such a free system as this there is a need for personification (e.g., God, Devil). If God's nature were less flexible, he might be above possessing the attributes of personality, just as many have imagined him to be. As it is, we have projected the known and the felt destructive forces into the idea of the Devil, and then consolidated all of these positive and negative forces into the concept of God. It is necessary to do this in order to see how all these factors relate to one another. Or more accurately, we want to see how they might all be related in various ways, so that we can discern what it is that holds them together in any unison at all.

No decision can be reached without that concentration of attributes, the loose unity of which constitutes personality, and this means that a free system is not free to rise above personification at the core of its first principles. Where God is not personified, we often need to reject God in order to prevent an intrusion and the overriding of an alien power on man's personality. However, according to the view outlined above, we cannot have an original creative action in a free system without the qualities of personality being operative. It is no longer necessary to reject God in the name of freedom. In fact, it is necessary to

163

have his decisive action first. Only as a result of divine free action can man have a context in which to be, and to be free.

It is not possible for a nonpersonal principle to allow a person to be free. A suprapersonal principle, such as Tillich's "Ground of Being," might provide this; it is just that we cannot be sure about it. It is possible for one person to allow another person to exercise his freedom. Of course, he does not have to do this, and men often do not allow it in fact, but they may. At least freedom is humanly possible between men. We constantly encroach on the freedom of other men. Indeed, when acting in relation to other human beings, it is impossible to be or to act without restricting in some degree either the action or the thought of others.

God could not act in creation without setting certain limits on the range of action left open as possible to men. Otherwise men could not act at all, that is, if they did not exist within some particular structure. However, God is capable of withholding his interference and of maintaining a "hands-off" policy, although nothing restricts him from interfering except the power of his own will in backing his rational decision. Men are capable of not interfering with the action and thought of others, but their powers of restraint are considerably less trustworthy. Our lack of self-sufficiency continually forces us toward intervention, since often we are willing to restrict freedom in the hope of gaining increased stability. Freedom is impossible without external and internal stability, and yet this also tends to turn and inhibit free action.

If man is free, is there any sense in which he still needs God? We will not answer this question on the religious level, although it might be an important consideration, but only consider God in relation to freedom. Intellectually speaking, a free man needs God only in order to understand his freedom, its conditions, its limits, and its possible alternatives. By exploration man can learn about this "from the inside," but nothing except God can explain to him why his freedom has the specific limits it has. This is because God's free action, and not simple possibility, defines our limits, so that it is God's action we most need to understand.

This is important because one of our most common errors in

exercising freedom is to think its range is greater than it is. Sometimes today we even make the mistake of identifying freedom with an absence of all limits and a lack of all restraint. Or sometimes we confuse our situation with a range of freedom which in fact man does not possess, simply because God did not select that form originally. Freedom is understood, i.e., its limits are set, by discerning God's intention in creation.

The details of what we are free to do or not to do in any situation come from an understanding of that context. Sometimes we are unclear about our mode of freedom itself. Then, to understand the conditions under which God elected our order may be the only way not to confuse our limits with those which are either wider or narrower in range than our world in fact allows. To exceed the limits of our power is to fail in our action and cause destruction in the futile attempt. To underestimate the range open to us is to fall into lethargy and fail to do what we can.

The concept of God within which we operate sets our range of freedom for us. In order to understand what our type of freedom includes and excludes, we also need to understand the relation between God and the Devil, because free action is often stopped when the enemy is underestimated. Knowledge has accomplished its goal only when both the positive and negative forces are understood precisely as they are balanced in a personality, and only then does free action become possible, since it must work its way between the opposing forces. Effective action must also borrow the power of the forces present in a situation in order to implement its aim. *Freedom fails to accomplish that delicate task unless it understands how Nonbeing underlies Being and how facing the Devil can lead to God.*

Not every force, of course, has been analyzed or included in this account. Love or compassion might be central in a creative first principle, but that fact only becomes clear in an attempt to solve the problem of evil positively, and this is a matter which is left open at this point.* What has emerged is not a complete concept of God but a tendency to move in certain directions that

*For one attempt to ask and answer the question of evil, see my *God, Why Did You Do That?* (Philadelphia: Westminster Press, 1970).

will determine how metaphysical principles are defined. From this I have selected certain further suggestions around which to build the basis for a concept of God. In order to be adequate, more detail would be necessary. Atheism should not and cannot provide that. In our day it merely points out the direction in which we ought to turn to begin to form a concept of God that can hope to be adequate in dealing with the arguments against it.

The problem of atheism is more real than the question of God's nature, and in any day it makes sense to try to find God where the questions are most pressing. Whenever some earlier uncertainty has been resolved and then given specific form in a doctrine, the result is satisfactory for that generation, but recovering such insight is almost bound to be blocked in a later time. This is because our tendency is to accept clear conclusions but to fail to grasp the confusion of forces which probably first called forth that definite answer by inducing a reaction against them.

In our time atheism is forceful, and around it much confusion swirls. These are healthy conditions, that is, if from them new insight can come to draw meaning out of what threatens to become intellectual chaos. If you begin negatively, you do not find as a result one and only one concept of God, but at least you do meet a God who is likely to be able to encounter and withstand the strong forces of evil present in the hour. What more than that can man ask from a concept of God in any day?

Concluding Postscript:
Never Trust a God over Thirty

The slogan of today's younger generation, "Never trust a man over thirty," may have a slightly bizarre sound when it is applied to God. Yet, if we consider this application, it may have a beneficial effect on our thinking about both man and God.

If our college-age revolutionaries think that anyone over thirty is hopelessly committed to the "establishment" and thus can neither understand the problems of youth nor free himself to solve them, think how old and tired and hopelessly committed a God would be who had been around since eternity! This issue is not humorous but serious. Of course, we have learned that what we deal with are concepts of God and not God himself, except as he may be experienced through and by means of some vital concept. The issue is this: Do our concepts of God grow old and become involved, so that eventually they are no longer free nor have the power to meet the needs of a new generation?

In our day of atheism there is some evidence that this is true. There are, certainly, technical reasons why a concept of God cannot stay young indefinitely, which have already been pointed out; but why is it that in our day the problem of finding a youthful concept of God has become so all-important?

The forces that argue for atheism almost always rest part of their argument on the irrelevance of an ancient God as measured against the needs of contemporary man. If we follow the lines of some classical model, our usual tendency is to think of God as timeless, but today the issue seems to be like this: Can we learn *maybe why Jesus died at 33— unless 85.*

to think about God as eternally young and as never passing thirty? Today's younger generation will, of course, all too soon find itself on the other side of thirty. Wouldn't it be just slightly funny if only God were able continually to stay under thirty? In this case not God but only man would grow old and tired. Set in his ways, thus man alone would lose the vigor and flexibility of youth.

Maybe, then, we have lost God in the modern age because we have let him grow old, and because we have tried to preserve a concept of him when it is past its prime. Perhaps the theological lesson we learn from today's demonstrating and revolutionary student generation is that the only way worth thinking about God is as if he were constantly able to maintain his youth.

Anyone who deals daily with young people in a college situation both sees and feels the assets of youth. On the whole the young are not afraid of major decisions, and they make changes of momentous consequence as if they could always be done over again the next day. Their minds are flexible; they are able to adapt easily to novelty and to new situations. They clearly feel the power of their freedom of will to effect change, and they rebel against an older generation's assertion that old orders have to be as in fact they are. The young have an ability to identify and understand both ideas and people who by nature and circumstance are quite different from themselves. For youth the lines that define inequality are not yet fixed, and all students are equals. Pure democracy is a natural youthful instinct. They accept freely and are accepted everywhere without intruding the question of status. To be young means not yet to be identified with any one limited structure that marks you, that separates you from others, and which you must defend as a means to preserve your form of life.

We all know the faults of the young; perhaps no one is more aware of them than disillusioned and unromantic youth. God, in order to be God, would have to avoid these pitfalls; he would have to be a *perfect youth*. That is, he should maintain the flexible virtues and the freedom of the young and yet not be subject to the quixotic changes and instabilities that accompany them in man. Whatever the faults of youth and whatever our ability to

168

correct them, a concept of God drawn on the model of "under thirty" has much to recommend itself in our day.

Naturally this calls for a revolution in our way of thinking about God, but then many revolutions in thought are called for nowadays. For instance, such a youthful God could not be entirely above time; he would have to involve himself in it. Not that he needs to be completely subject to the confines of time as we are. We perhaps escape time in our thought, but the possession of abundant youthful energy would be bound to move God into time occasionally. He might, of course, tolerate the "establishment," since he created at least its possibility, but he would not identify himself with any one form of created human structure.

What happens to all our antique concepts of God if, now having passed thirty, they are no longer to be trusted? If we consider this question, we also discover a moral to be drawn as far as men over thirty are concerned. That is, if an honorable past is not automatically to be given leadership in the present hour, at least it ought not to be ignored in our education. Each of these old men and old ideas of God were once young, and what we want to learn about them is this: "What were they like in their youth; how did they achieve their strength and use it in an earlier hour of crisis in order to preserve order and create value?"

By turning our attention to the time when what is now old was once young, we may see that nothing begins by being old. What we need to learn, then, is the "secret of constant youth," and understanding God may provide us with our only access to the long-sought-for fountain of youth. How can what once was young and vital maintain that youthful vigor and flexibility? Can we revive the youth still left in either the ancient concept or the old society? Can that which tends to age renew itself and become young again?

If this is possible, then "age" and "youth" are not matters strictly connected to chronological sequence. Whenever we list the desirable features of youth, we immediately see that not everyone under thirty possesses them all, and that some old men have learned the secret of staying young at least in attitude and in outlook. Perhaps this is the true picture of God: he is not beyond time, but rather possesses the secret of constant youth,

169

I like that concept of an eternal life — I heaven to

i.e., has the power for a renewal of vitality without ceasing. ✗

Such a God always remains under thirty, and only men slip on toward old age. In him there is constant vitality and flexibility. If so, there is no need to clutch at established ways in order to gain security. Now we can have a God with the constant freedom of youth and with its adaptability. Here is the source of renewal; here is a God who can change and move easily from the highest to the lowest. It is possible for old men to stay young; those who cannot are not dependable. On the other hand, a God who always maintains himself under thirty is one who can always be trusted.

It takes youth to oppose the evil of destruction that comes when the Devil appears. In order to resist this force, man needs to trust in a God always "under thirty." At the height of this battle against evil, God may appear as young again and as never old. Apparently this is the only way in which atheism can be overcome, and in that struggle either God is rediscovered in fresh form or else he is lost from sight.

For the TRUMPET of God is a blessed intelligence and so are all the instruments in HEAVEN
For God the father Almighty plays upon a HARP of stupendous magnitude and melody.
For at that time malignity ceases and the devils themselves are at peace.
For this time is perceptible to man by a remarkable stillness and serenity of soul.

christopher smart,
in JUBILATE AGNO

170

Index

INDEX

70 71 72 73 10 9 8 7 6 5 4 3 2 1